A Member of
the Family

A Member of the Family

Strategies for Black Family Continuity

Ann Creighton Zollar

Nelson-Hall Publishers  Chicago

LIBRARY OF CONGRESS CATALOGING IN PUBLICATION DATA

Zollar, Ann Creighton.
  A member of the family.

  Bibliography: p.
  Includes index.
  1. Afro-American families. 2. Afro-Americans—Social
conditions—1975–   . I. Title.
E185.86.Z65 1985   305.8'96073   84–6849
ISBN 0–8304–1031–7

Manufactured in the United States of America

10 9 8 7 6 5 4 3 2 1

The paper in this book is pH neutral (acid-free).

To all *black families*

Contents

Chapter 1
Introduction

RECENT months have witnessed not only a proliferation
of predictions about the impact of the Reagan adminis-
tration's fiscal retrenchment on black families but also
suggestions about how blacks must "cope" with the situation. Among these suggestions have been those that insist that blacks must once again draw upon the strengths
of the extended family, which "has served them so well
in the past." Though these suggestions indicate a certain
awareness of black history, they also indicate a lack of insight into the organization of many contemporary urban
black families and a naivete about the ability of extended
family structures to withstand strain.

In this book I describe four contemporary urban
black families as they were organized in 1978–1979 and
three of them as they existed in 1982.* These two sets of

---

*A report of the methodology and findings of this research appeared in a
condensed form as an article in the 1982 Fall issue of *The Western Journal of
Black Studies.*

observations allow a reasoned assessment of how these families have changed over four years and may strengthen future attempts to ferret out which changes in the families can be attributed to political and economic changes in the wider society by providing a baseline for study which existed prior to the current and widely acknowledged "crisis."[1]

Just as the past few months have seen increasing forecasts about how proposed changes in federal policy will affect black families, the immediate future will surely hold controversies surrounding the validity of complex models used to measure that impact and the reliability of government data plugged into them. Once the focus of the controversy has shifted to numbers, it will be difficult to bring it back to people. Concern about the impact of "Reaganomics" on broad statistical categories is, of course, legitimate. The situation cannot be understood, however, without taking into account families such as those discussed here. At this point only the media have turned their attention to people, and they have been accused of being economically and politically motivated to seek out and present only the most extreme cases.[2] The structure of the present work at least avoids that criticism.

The research reported on here was conducted while I was a fellow of the National Fellowship Fund for Black Americans. It was designed to identify and describe, in micro-detail, some contemporary urban black families. My thesis is that though the black family has been viewed as the locus of past, present, and future social problems, those structures and/or processes which are the black family have yet to be adequately conceptualized and/or empirically delineated. As several authors have pointed out, the traditional theoretical approaches to the study of black family life have been complicated by the presence of both objective (conceptual framework) and subjective (ideological perspective) components (Allen, 1978; Dodson, 1981; Johnson, 1981; Mathis, 1978; Staples, 1978). The goal of this research required that the objective component of the approach involved be a derivative of systems analysis. Billingsley (1968) has already outlined the utility of a systems approach to the study of black family life. He defines a system as "an organization of units or elements united in some form of regular interaction and interdependence . . . it has boundaries which allow us to distinguish the internal from the external environment, and it is typically embedded in a network of social units both larger and smaller than itself" (Billingsley, 1968:4).

According to Billingsley, consideration of the black family as a social system leads to understanding that black social mobility is closely intertwined with the course of social change within both the black community and the wider society. In carrying out this study, it quickly became apparent that the nature and location of boundaries was an essential part of the problem. Attempts to adopt the systems approach to the needs of the study resulted in understanding that where and by whom the familial boundaries were to be drawn must be treated as an ideological problem of the first magnitude.

Allen (1978) describes three ideological perspectives on the black family: (1) the cultural deviant; (2) the cultural equivalent; and (3) the cultural variant. These headings can be used to discuss the implications of boundary drawing.[3]

The view of the black family as culturally deviant has

been fairly well crystalized as the "Old Model" (Lieberman, 1973). This model of the black family in American society included the notions that the black family was one monolithic lower-class entity, that it was dominated by females, characterized by high rates of "illegitimacy" and marital dissolution, and produced males with low self-esteem. It was in and of itself a social problem.

The emergence of a perspective which views the black family as culturally equivalent to white families involved attempts to refute the simplistic assumptions of the old model. Whereas the old model identified the black family as one monolithic lower-class entity, developers of the equivalence perspective emphasized the variety found in black families. Billingsley (1968) identified twelve structural types, geographically distributed in urban/rural areas and Northern/Southern locations and differentiated by social class.

Once the existence of variety among black families became an accepted framework, social class gained prominence as the explanatory variable. When confronted with evidence that black familial practices and behavior differ from those of whites, proponents of the equivalence perspective often suggest that black-white familial differences are explainable primarily in terms of social class. The idea that power in the black family was concentrated within females was countered by research reports which indicated that when social class is controlled, the role structure of black families is not dissimilar to that found in white families (Hyman and Reed, 1969; Mack, 1974; TenHouten, 1970). Similarly, the notion that the absent father typified black families was refuted by studies that showed that the influence of income was far greater than that of ethnicity (Blumberg and Garcia,

1977). Although there are several versions of this perspective, the general argument contends that blacks are disproportionately represented in the lower class, and it is this overrepresentation that gives the impression of a special type of family life among blacks.

According to Allen (1978), proponents of the view that sees black families as culturally variant criticize the equivalence perspective for its tendency to de-emphasize or negate those qualities of black family life that are distinctive. From the culturally variant perspective, those same qualities represent valid expressions of Afro-American cultural forms. At one level, this perspective implies that it is the existence of a viable black culture which accounts for the observable differences between black and white family patterns. At another level, it implies that even those characteristics of black families which are similar to white families have been achieved through different processes, styles of interaction, and qualities of personal relationships. The proponents of this perspective argue that the goal of the sociologist who studies the black family should not be to react to negative images of the black family but rather to look beneath its surface and describe and analyze the unique characteristics of black family life.

Allen (1978) goes on to suggest that researchers should select the ideological perspective most suited to their research problem. For the problem at hand, this eliminates both the cultural deviant and the cultural equivalent perspectives. As divergent as these two perspectives are they tend to have certain similarities when it comes to drawing boundaries for black families. Both of these approaches to the study of black family life have been unduly constrained by a reliance on common residence as the empirical identifier of families (Winch, 1977) and the conjugal bond as the primary organizing principle (Aschenbrenner, 1975; Sudarkasa, 1981).

In some instances the household concept has been used to describe black families. Though there are some advantages associated with this practice, they are far outweighed by the disadvantages. The major advantage of utilizing the household concept is that it allows the exploitation of available data collected through regular periodic surveys. The primary example of such data is that collected by the United States Census of Population. Every national census has collected data on households (Winch, 1977) and classified the population by race or color (Farley, 1970).

While reasonably accurate census data may provide a wealth of knowledge about the family system of a group or country, it must be interpreted with caution. In some cases household composition may be more reflective of urban housing conditions and levels of poverty than indicative of the type of family system. At least part of the logic behind utilizing the household concept as a unit of analysis lies in its importance as an empirically identifiable ecological and economic unit. "It consists of those persons who, so to speak, put their feet under the same table, or otherwise join together in an arrangement to provide food, shelter, and other basic residential necessities" (Bogue, 1969:368). Ethnographic research has suggested that, among low-income urban blacks, feet may not be put under the table in quite this fashion. Rather than being the simple concrete units often assumed, black households have been found to exhibit multiple and shifting memberships (Stack, 1974; Valentine, 1978).

It has even been suggested that it may not be possible to determine to which household an individual belongs or, conversely, to determine the membership of each housing unit. "A resident in the Flats who eats in one household may sleep in another, and contribute resources to yet another. He may consider himself a member of all three households" (Stack, 1974:31). It is not necessary, however, to conclude that the household is a meaningless unit of analysis. There are advantages in utilizing the household concept to discuss the relational aspects of black family life. The notion of "residential flux," if it is not considered an *a priori* indicator of disorganization, deserves and invites study. We must ask, for example, what are the factors which determine the household compositions resulting from the expansions, contractions, and successive recombinations of kin living together.

Gonzalez (1970) has suggested that we treat the individual described above as a member of all three households, modifying the view of households as closed bonded units. This view also recognizes that individuals can have simultaneous loyalties to more than one residential group.

Since 1947 the Bureau of the Census has attempted to distinguish between families and households (Lammermeier, 1973). A household has been defined as consisting of all the persons who share a dwelling unit. A house, an apartment, even a single room, if occupied as separate living quarters, is considered to be a household. A family, on the other hand, has been defined as consisting of those persons who are related to each other by blood, marriage, or adoption, and who share the same household (Bogue, 1969).

In the study of black families in American society the important problems that arise from confusion of the concepts of household and family are not those that arise from confusion of the two terms as defined above. Single-person households, households composed of unrelated persons, and those who live in group quarters are seldom treated as families. Also, it is generally well recognized that two or more families may occupy the same household. The problems that do arise center around whether those social structures and/or processes that are the black family can be empirically identified or adequately conceptualized in terms of shared residence.

The failure to consistently recognize that "residence" is what is referred to by "household" while the referent of "family" is "kinship" leads to both empirical and conceptual problems. Using the household concept to describe black families and/or defining them on the basis of a shared residency requirement have a similar disadvantage. Neither explanation can provide any insight into familial systems which transcend household boundaries.

Use of the terms "family" and "household" as though they were interchangeable results in the myth of the female-headed black family. This involves both a tendency on the part of scholars to confuse a statistically significant fact, the presence of some female-headed households, with the typical or characteristic domestic arrangement (Gutman, 1976) and the tendency to confuse this domestic arrangement with the family. "I am not here employing the word 'myth' in its present popular meaning of something widely believed and contrary to fact, but rather in its earlier sense, as a metaphor of some subtlety on a subject difficult to describe in any other way'' (Sagan, 1977:8).

The key to transcending the myth lies in understanding that the difficult is not the impossible and attempting to approach the black family from a perspective which is explicitly cognizant of the actual empirical relationship between households and families. The membership roster of empirically identifiable families and empirically locatable households may not coincide. In some cases this may occur because a member of the family is absent from the household (Ball, 1972). In other cases it may occur because ''the family'' transcends household boundaries.

Anthropologists studying kinship in Caribbean societies have long realized the need to distinguish between households (residential groups or domestic arrangements) and the family.[4] Typically they substitute for a definition of family that relies on common residence one that relies on the conjugal bond. Gonzalez (1969:84) first defines the family ''as a group of people bound together by kinship ties, between at least two of whom there exists a conjugal relationship recognized by the society in which they live'' (1969:84). She then presents the distinction between families and households to illustrate that among the Caribs this family could be spread over several different households without loss of affective bonds. The structure of the family as a kinship network is preserved through mutual concern, frequent visiting, and patterned reciprocity. Gutman (1976) has pointed out the utility of this same distinction in consideration of Afro-American slave families. The absence of a father in a household may have involved his belonging to a different master, but did not necessarily preclude affective cohesion even when frequent visiting was difficult.

Conceptual clarity does not seem to lie in focusing on the conjugal bond. Many discussions about the nature of black family life focus on the alleged frailty of the marital tie. "This emphasis reflects the overriding importance of the marital tie in our society, rather than any peculiarity of the black family. In societies with extended families, other relationships . . . may be more important in terms of social and economic support than that of husband and wife" (Aschenbrenner, 1975:3). Sudarkasa (1981) suggests in fact that among black Americans the principle of conjugality is subordinate to the principle of consanguinity, "that historically among Black Americans the concept of 'family' meant first and foremost relationships created by blood rather than marriage" (1981:69).

Since only the cultural variant perspective allows these issues to be explored by forcing the researcher to admit the possibility of boundaries other than those provided for in the nuclear family model, it appeared an ideal perspective from which to undertake this study. Therefore, I began this research in 1978 without designating any collectivity of persons, roles, or statuses as the proper referent of the term "family." Instead, I imposed both structural and functional criteria and identified as a family sets of individuals, the relations among whom bore designations of kinship and who engaged in a system of mutual aid involving the exchange of goods and services.

Based on the outcome of this research, I have undertaken the writing of this book for three major reasons. First, many blacks, no matter what their economic situations, will be unable to "return" to the extended family pattern, because involvement with the extended kin is a way of life that they have never abandoned. Using the procedures outlined in chapter 2, I identified four contemporary urban black families as they existed in 1978 and 1979. Each of the four families already had an external structure most adequately captured by the term "extended." In each case, that group of individuals whose relationships bore designations of kinship and who participated in a system of mutual aid involving the exchange of goods and services, spanned three to four generations and was spread out over several households. The descriptions of these families, in minute detail, are presented in chapters 3 to 6 and form the core of this work. The major portion of these descriptions remain largely unchanged from the way I wrote them in 1980. In three cases, however, I have been able to supplement these descriptions with a discussion of how the family was organized in 1982.

Second, black extended families are by no means identically organized nor are they identically prepared to deal with adverse changes in their political and economic environment. Some black extended families continue to possess untapped resources. Others are already functioning at their maximum capability, using every organizational and economic resource available to them in order to survive. In chapter 7 I discuss the differences in these families as well as their commonalities. I also explore the implications of these commonalities and differences for the continuity of the family.

Third, it remains necessary to debunk the myth which claims that black involvement with the extended kin represents an adaptation to conditions of urban poverty. In chapter 8 I discuss the origin of this myth. I also ask how can it be true when kin involvement and mutual aid persist after some degree of prosperity has been reached and when recent sociohistorical treatments of the development of Afro-American family patterns emphasize the role played by the extended family pattern in insuring that enslaved Africans survived to become black "Americans."

In chapter 9 attention is turned to explaining and describing how extended kinship survives in the urban environment. I look first at the development of the black community in Chicago with emphasis on how the disruptive effects of economic differentiation on kinship organization have been mediated through the emergence and stabilization of residential segregation. Finally, I turn attention to how black families existing in urban environments transmit from generation to generation the knowledge that sharing between and among kin constitutes appropriate behavior.

Chapter 2
Identifying the Families

THE design of my original study called for an attempt to emulate the social anthropologist, who pitches a tent in the middle of a native village and proceeds to observe and record what is actually going on. With this goal in mind, I moved into Chicago's Austin Community area. From the beginning I realized that I should not attempt to generalize from the small number of black families I would be able to observe to all black families or to "The Black Family." My primary concern was with maximizing the number of observations I would be able to make of each family and the "naturalness" of the situations under which I would be able to observe. I also planned to use statistical information to describe the area in which the families lived and to attempt to determine if the families identified were typical of families in the community area. I also realized that I would not be facing the problems of the cultural outsider, but those of the insider. My problems would not include gaining an entree into the lives of people without knowing anything about their patterns or meaning of life. My problems would revolve around becoming so immersed in the lives of people that I was oblivious to the fact that patterns do exist.

I had no difficulty locating potential informants in Austin. No one questioned my right to live there or to ask them questions about their daily lives. What the informants in Austin did question was my right not to be totally involved, and involved in a manner that they perceived as consistent with easily observable researcher characteristics. To those potential informants who lived nearby I was primarily a female heading a household containing herself and two children with no regularly visiting man or kin. Though I was not being supported by welfare, my new neighbors quickly and accurately recognized that I was "just as poor as everybody else."[1] They were reluctant to accept someone with my primary characteristics as a bona fide researcher. While I was trying to get them to respond to my inquiries about their family lives some of my new neighbors were trying to find me a man and/or a family and others were trying to exploit my vulnerability.[2]

While living in Austin I did learn quite a lot about what it means to be a poor black female heading a household and isolated from kin. This information, however, was of little use in addressing the questions that I had set out to answer. Since I had no intention of changing the research problem and was much too poor to simply select a more congenial research site, I changed my methods of securing informants.

I decided that the best way to select informants who would see my claim to the researcher role as a valid one was by having a third party introduce me to them. Through the efforts of a faculty member I was introduced to four recent graduates of the high school located in Austin who were involved with a youth service agency. I was introduced to them as a student from "Circle"[3] who was interested in studying black families and who would appreciate their cooperation. At our first meeting each of these young people agreed to participate in the study. By the time I contacted them a second time, however, they had come to realize that "there was nothing in it for them" and that no one would force them to help me. Only one of them, a young, single male, was even willing to sit through the first interview. I refer to this young man as "Kicker" because it was he who kicked this study off by proving the profile for subsequent informants. Other acquaintances were then asked to introduce me to young, single, black males who had been "raised" on welfare.

The initial informant from each family described here was chosen because he fit a particular profile rather than because he lived in a particular area of the city. I was introduced to a score of young men before I found the four whose families are presented here and without whose cooperation this work would not have been possible. Only one of them lived near me in Austin, and he is the only one that I can claim to have discovered myself. Each of these young men was asked to participate in an interview process. From them I collected a spontaneous listing of relatives and a genealogy, which together provided the primary slate of candidates for inclusion within the family.

For each relative placed in the genealogy the informant was asked to supply an age and an address. For each adult he was asked to estimate the number of years of school completed and the monthly income. In addition, he was asked to identify the person's source of income and to describe how often and under what circumstances he interacted with that person. Those relatives about whom the informant had a great deal of knowledge and with whom he interacted on a regular basis were termed "intimate kin" and became a second less-inclusive slate of candidates for family membership. The informant was then asked to introduce me to his intimate kin. The set of interviews was then conducted with them until overlapping listings of intimate kin were found. This last step was important because each respondent/informant sometimes drew his or her intimate kin from distinct pools of relatives who had little knowledge about and even less contact with each other.

The lists of overlapping intimate kin and the information gathered about them during the interview process provided more than data to be stored away and analyzed at some later date. The data gathered in these initial interviews were also the lists of characters needed to begin firsthand observations. The lists allowed the researcher to ask questions about and understand conversations about relatives in their absence. The administering of the innocuous interviews also served to solidify my role as researcher, since everyone knows that researchers "do interviews."

By the time the interviews had been administered to three intimately related individuals (no later than a month after initial contact and generally including the initial informant, his mother, and his maternal grandmother) some person or persons had been found who could tolerate the presence of the researcher without a set interview format. These individuals managed to make it quite clear that they would be more than willing to help me identify and describe their families. I made arrangements with these individuals to visit with them in their homes, to be present when relatives came to visit them, and to go with them when they went to visit relatives. These rounds of visits often involved showing up with a diagram like those found in the following pages and asking those present whether or not it included everyone they considered to be a member of the family. In some cases the discussions surrounding who was "in" and who was "out" of a family lasted throughout the entire research process. Nevertheless, in each of these cases there was a tipping point, a point at which enough people had been interviewed, enough households visited, and enough babies kissed for the researcher to decide that an empirically existing black family had been identified. From this point on it was no longer necessary to ask specific questions about occupation, income, or genealogical connection. The point had been reached when I could show up at a household unaccompanied by another relative and be met at the door by people reciting their genealogies and telling me "their side of the story."

In most instances what came out in the sessions where individuals told me "their side of the story" was an explanation of why their relationships with their kin were or were not what they should be. Once each member of the family who wanted to and/or was willing to had delivered these explanations, it was possible to extensively observe their behavior toward and with kin.

I never attempted to become a member of these families. They always knew that when I was around I was observing. Yet for more than a year I was not only allowed but often encouraged to join in and to observe them as they went about their daily activities. And while it may sound like the age old apologia of the fieldworker to say that how I observed, how much I observed, and what I observed varied with each case, it is nevertheless true. As I visited with the members of these families I attempted to follow them through their daily activities. I observed from the fixing or not fixing of breakfast in the morning to the saying or not saying of prayers at night. I tagged along to the grocery store, the liquor store, the utility companies, and the schools. I went with them to the welfare office, the hospital, the airport, the bar, the restaurant, and all the other places that "lower-class" black people in urban America go. I followed the planning of and attended as many of each family's special events as possible. I went to baby showers, weddings, birthday and anniversary parties, Tupperware parties, and jewelry demonstrations. I attended going-away parties, coming-home parties, and just-because-we-want-to-and-we-can parties.

During the initial interview period I focused on who belonged to the family and tried to get them to show me where the boundaries were actually drawn. In the 1978–1979 observation period I concentrated on trying to understand who did what for whom, how often they did it, what they expected, and what they got in return. In writing up each case I tried to focus on a single family member who had been "mobile." This particular focus demands an explanation of how an individual who is "merely stably employed" can be defined as having experienced mobility. Perception of this situation is difficult due to the general tendency to view the black lower class as a homogeneous mass despite the fact that Billingsley (1968) and others have pointed out that the black lower class is more aptly viewed as three broad layers: the working nonpoor, the working poor, and the nonworking poor. Billingsley referred to this last layer as the ''underclass'' and visualized them as being both below and outside of the conventional American class structure.[4]

Any attempt to estimate the size of the black underclass is necessarily arbitrary. Income, employment, and social welfare statistics can be used to both construct definitions and count the number of people who fall within this grouping. The Chicago Mayor's Office of Employment and Training estimated that 66 percent of the 586,000 city dwellers who qualified for CETA's job training program for the economically disadvantaged were black (Askin, 1980). The largest and most permanent segment of this disadvantaged population were welfare recipients. One observer of racial issues in Metropolitan Chicago has described the 350,000 children and almost 300,000 adult residents of Cook County who are dependent on welfare in the following fashion: ''Virtually all the children and about half the adults are receiving Aid to Families with Dependent Children (AFDC). One-third of AFDC adults have never held a job. One-third of AFDC families have been on welfare continuously for more than five years. . . . Few welfare recipients have the skills demanded for most well-paying jobs. Seventy percent never finished high school'' (Askin, 1980:3). For those within the underclass, obtaining and keeping any steady job must definitely be seen as upward mobility.

Families with roots and members in the underclass were selected as the ''objects'' of inquiry because for these families the questions raised here are of practical importance.

In 1982, I approached these families with the same

questions. Because the time I had to spend with them was much shorter, I relied more heavily on the information from unstructured interviews. Once again much of what I have to report about these families was gained by first-hand observation. Before these issues are discussed in analytical terms, however, I would like to introduce you to the Baker, Niles, Edmonds, and Jones families in such a way that their own words and actions allow you to understand how they are organized.[5]

Chapter 3
The Nileses

TWICE a week a Centennial Laundry truck passed my aunt's house on its way to return finished shirts to the small cleaners located at the corner of the one-way street on which she lives. Whenever she feels she can afford it, my aunt sends some younger member of the family ("Your legs are in better shape than mine") out to flag it down. One morning in the early fall of 1978, I was the selected truck flagger. While waiting for my aunt to finish stuffing her bag, the truck driver and I engaged in our usual chit-chat. Since he is also black and working on a degree, our conversations generally turned to school. On that morning I explained to him my need for informants who fit the profile set by Kicker.

Several days later my aunt called me at home to tell me that the truck driver had left a name and a number for me to try. When I dialed the number, the phone was answered by a female voice that I would soon learn to recognize as belonging to Tina Niles Murphy. When I asked to speak to Ryan, the name the truck driver had left for me, she explained that she was his mother and asked, "What has that boy done now?" I explained that I wasn't calling to report any wrongdoing of his, but rather to enlist his aid in my research project. "Oh yeah," she said, "Freddie [the truck driver] told me about you. If you want to catch Ryan, you'd better get here by two, 'cause that's as long as I can sit on him for you." I made it to Tina's house by one, and given the subsequent chain of events I was really glad that she had sat on Ryan for me.

That afternoon when I interviewed Ryan, he demonstrated quite a bit of knowledge about relatives to whom he was linked through his father as well as those to whom he was linked through his mother. I did not term any of Ryan's paternal kin "intimate relatives," because he hadn't been in regular contact with any of them for about ten years. Subsequently, I interviewed both his mother and his maternal grandmother, and it was their overlapping listings of intimate relatives who engaged in mutual aid that I termed the Niles family.

Before Christmas, however, Ryan and his younger brother Larry had moved to Omaha, Nebraska, to live with their father and his sister, forcing me to concentrate on the family that they had left behind. This family spanned three generations and five households.

In the Niles family the mobile individual on whom I concentrated was Tina Niles Murphy. Although Tina has at various times during her life been dependent upon welfare payments for support (even during her marriage to Ryan and Larry's father, Odie), she is now totally self-supporting. She works as a supervisor of directory assistance for Illinois Bell Telephone.

Tina interacts with some member of her family every day. She manages this interaction primarily through the telephone. She takes advantage of the free local calls allowed by her employer and spends much of her coffee break and lunch time chatting with friends and checking in with relatives. She generally saves visiting for days off. According to Tina, the greatest barrier to visiting is work schedules. Tina generally works weekends when the other members of her family are off from work, but she also generally works the swing shift (so named, she says, because it's for people who like to swing—and she does, going out almost every night after work).

When I first asked how often she visited her kin, Tina laughed and said, "According to my mother, not often enough." Although some of Tina's relatives live quite nearby, she visits with them only once or twice a month. She asks, "How can I visit them when we don't even live in the same part of the clock?"

According to Tina, the current residential proximity between her and her relatives is purely accidental. Until 1977, she was buying a small cottage in Roseland, some distance away from where any of her relatives live. She says that trying to purchase a single family home on her income was the second dumbest thing she has ever done (the first dumbest thing was marrying her first husband). Every paycheck, she says, had to be ploughed back into the house. One week the roof leaked, the next week the furnace was broken, two weeks later someone put a rock through the picture window. "Not only was I going out every night," she says, "but I was putting away plenty of booze while I was out there and feeling like an all-around shit."

Tina was already planning to get rid of the house

when she met her boyfriend, Edmond. When she explained to him how she felt about the house ("It was like I was going to work to support the damn thing instead of it providing me with a haven from the world"), he pointed out that he owned several apartment buildings, one of which needed a resident manager. After she looked at the place, she decided she liked it. The fact that she could have it rent free for performing such services as distributing light bulbs, calling plumbers and electricians, and making sure that they could gain access to the area where they were to work was very appealing. She claims that the fact that the apartment was closer to her relatives in no way influenced her decision to take it and that it has had no effect on the frequency with which she visits them. Her mother heartily concurs with the latter part of this statement.

Tina visits her mother more often than she visits any other member of her extended family. The person she visits next often is her sister Louise. Both Tina's mother, who is a supervisor of data processing for a large manufacturing firm, and her sister Louise, who is a registered nurse, make more money than Tina does. Tina laughs though, because she feels that Ma Bell has done "alright" by her.

When asked why she hardly ever visits her brother, Tina says that she let him live with her the last time he got out of jail and that was enough of his erratic behavior to last her for a long time. Besides, she said, "I simply cannot tolerate that woman he is married to."

When I asked Tina why she so seldom visited her sister Brenda, the only member of this family who was on welfare in 1978–1979, she laughed and pointed out that Brenda was only one year older than her own daughter

FIGURE 3.1.

The Niles family, September 1978.

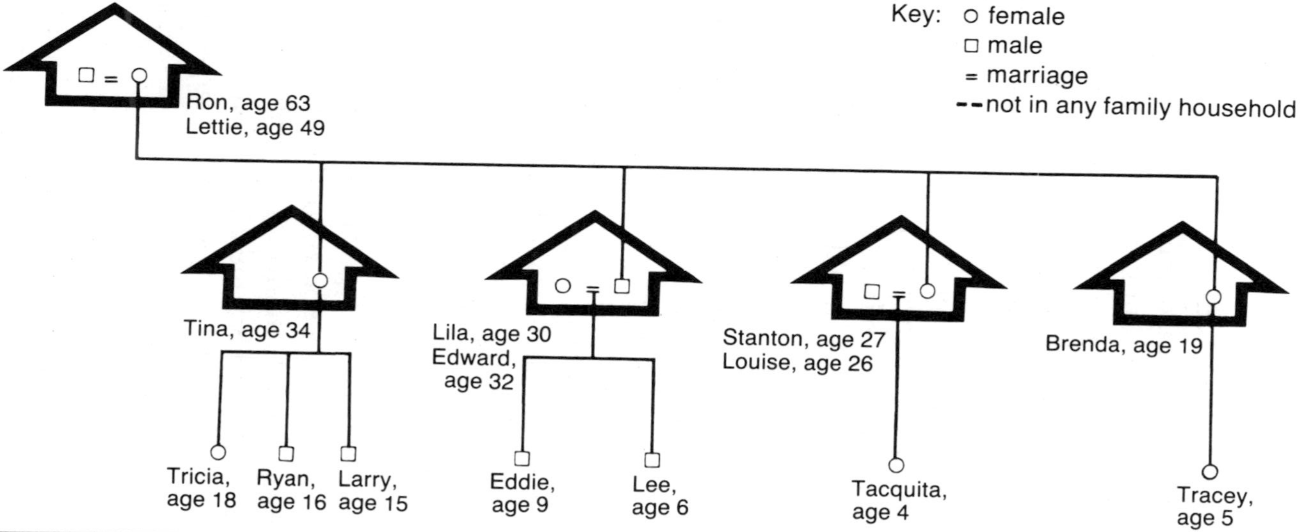

Key: ○ female
      □ male
      = marriage
      -- not in any family household

Ron, age 63
Lettie, age 49

Tina, age 34

Tricia,   Ryan,   Larry,
age 18   age 16   age 15

Lila, age 30
Edward,
age 32

Eddie,   Lee,
age 9   age 6

Stanton, age 27
Louise, age 26

Tacquita,
age 4

Brenda, age 19

Tracey,
age 5

Tricia. "When would I get a chance to visit with her? Half the time she is over here with Tricia, the other half of the time they are out in the street together."

Tina and her mother take turns visiting one another on a fairly equal basis. Tina refers to her mother's visits as "tours of inspection." One Saturday I went to Tina's house, and about twenty minutes later her mother showed up unannounced. Her mother was not there very long—in fact she never even sat down—and the only part of the conversation I was able to hear was the mother, Lettie, saying "You should clean up this house. It is a disgrace."

Tina's relatives don't visit with each other any more frequently than Tina visits them, and they tend to congregate only on holidays and for ritual occasions. In general, they express no desire for more frequent visiting. Tina's sister Louise in fact complains that her in-laws visit too much. "Every time I turn around there's some of them people on my front doorstep. I get so tired of them that sometimes I don't even open the door." And even Tina's mother, who complains that her children should come and visit her more often, admits that she gets upset only if they do not show up on holidays and occasions when she has made special arrangements or preparations for them. On those occasions there are generally outsiders present, and the festivities are confined to her large and well-appointed basement recreation room. The only two members of this family who spend large amounts of time with each other are the nineteen-year-old aunt, Brenda, and Tricia.

Brenda, in fact, claims to be the biggest visitor in the family. She also admits that her visits have a practical purpose. Since her welfare check is long gone before the end of the month, she often feeds herself and her small daughter by timing her arrivals at the homes of her kin to coincide with meal times. It is not unusual for her to have breakfast at her mother's, lunch at Louise's, and then show up at Tina's for dinner. The members of the family express awareness of the reasons behind Brenda's visits and even admit to doing their grocery shopping with her tastes in mind.

Neither does Brenda have to look far to find a baby-sitter. Her sister Louise is generally more than willing to keep her daughter, Tracey. Louise says that the big back-yard behind her single family home is a much better place for Tracey to play than the inside of Brenda's studio apartment. She also claims that Tracey makes good company for her own daughter, Tacquita. One of the favorite jokes in the Niles family involves the mix-matchedness of these two sisters and their daughters. Brenda, at five feet, ten inches, is a lithe dark-skinned beauty, whose physical characteristics are more clearly reflected in her dark skinny niece, Tacquita, than in her own daughter. Tracey, on the other hand, with a short body that is all soft, round plumpness and a "high yellow" complexion, looks like a small replica of her Aunt Louise.

Brenda admits that along with her meals she has to be willing to stomach the lectures that her family passes out. According to Brenda, her mother's favorite lecture is, "Why couldn't you have been more like Louise?" Louise, according to her mother, was always a quiet and demure child, who went through high school in record time and with grades good enough to win herself a four-year college scholarship. Louise majored in nursing and had been working as an R.N. for two years before she met and married Stanton, her policeman husband. Their first child, Tacquita, was born two years after the marriage.

Tina argues that Brenda should learn from her (Tina's) experience. According to Tina, when she was sixteen years old, she was the mother of a one-year-old child and still trying to finish high school when the world collapsed around her. Her mother had grown tired of trying to care for four children on ADC payments and irregular contributions by their father, who worked everyday but never could make it home sober or with paycheck intact. When Lettie met a man some years her senior who offered her a secure home and a chance to go back to school on the condition that she leave not only her husband but also her two oldest children, she simply packed up and left. Tina and Edward were then left to negotiate through the world on their own.

While Lettie was studying data processing, moving up the ladder at her place of employment, and making joint real estate investments with her new husband, Edward was in and out of jail and Tina was running around the street and not thinking much about the future. When Tina became pregnant with Ryan, she and Odie were married. Less than twelve months after the birth of Ryan, Larry was born. Odie had left her and the children in a run-down rooming house with the rent past due. She followed him to Omaha, but he treated her badly, openly running around with other women, refusing to give her money for food and clothes, and beating her when she protested. Therefore, she moved back to Chicago and began to make plans. First she applied for welfare, then found a job working the night shift in a Zenith factory. Every week, even though Odie had come back to live with her, she put some money in the bank for a divorce.

For a while, in order to make ends meet, she had to work two jobs—the night shift at Zenith and a day job at Spiegel's (a Chicago mail-order house). It was, she remembers, one of her co-workers at Spiegel's who first alerted her to the fact that the phone company was hiring directory assistance operators and encouraged her to apply. She applied, was hired, and has been there ever since. Tina is not reluctant to admit that though she has been with the phone company for slightly more than ten years, it was only four years ago that her income from working exceeded the limit for supplemental assistance from public aid. All in all, however, she feels that she has done a good job of standing on her "own two feet," and constantly suggests to her younger sister that she should do the same.

The entire family, as a matter of fact, has begun to warn Brenda that the one-way flow of goods and services to her may soon cease if she does not "get herself together." Tina, Louise, and their brother and mother have offered to pool their resources in such a manner that she can go to school and learn some trade or skill which would allow her to be self-supporting.

In helping each other, the Niles constantly express a preference for a mutual aid system which operates in times of crisis and which emphasizes large, one-time-only projects. Mrs. Niles in fact explains that Brenda's being on welfare represents a constant state of crisis, which, if she could gain steady employment, might become only intermittent. If, she goes on to explain, the employment for Brenda were adequate rather than just steady, then the whole family could breathe a collective sigh of relief and concentrate their efforts on the next generation. She uses Tina as an example of this type of mobility.

Soon after Tina began working for the phone company she became dissatisfied with public housing. According to Tina, the low rent that she paid to live in Chicago's Stateway Gardens did not compensate for the fear that she felt every time she got on the elevator or the even greater fear when the elevator was out of order and she had to venture into stairwells darkened by the broken, stolen, or burned out light bulbs. When someone broke into her apartment while she was at work one night, without even waking up her sleeping children, she decided it was time to move.

First she tried apartments. Those apartments she could afford and where the landlord was willing to rent to a single mother with three children were no more to her liking than the project had been. Everyone in the family repeats the story of how they came to the aid of a sorely pressed Tina when she was looking for an apartment. Tina had looked at an apartment in West Garfield. When the landlord agreed to make certain repairs and decorate she gave him a month's rent as deposit and promised to pay the first month's rent the following payday. When payday came Tina went to the office early, picked up her check, and went to cash it. She didn't have time to go to the new apartment before work, so waited until she got off that night. Since she had informed housing that she was moving the next day, she was anxious to give the new landlord the money. When she got to the new apartment she discovered that not only had the landlord not done any of the work he had promised, but vandals had broken in and made an even worse mess of the place. Tina began the bus ride home thinking that at least she had the money to pay CHA, and they wouldn't throw her out if the rent was paid. When she got home, however, she discovered that she had lost the small coin purse in which she had been carrying the money. Tired, disgusted, and filled with thoughts of having no place to live, Tina called her family.

Tina's brother Edward came over and together they retraced her CTA routes. They looked on buses, talked to bus drivers, and went to the barns on each route. They found no trace of the purse. When they got back to the apartment in Stateway Gardens the sun was already up and Tina discovered that her mother, sisters, and children had finished her packing for her. She didn't understand what was going on until she saw her stepfather drive up in a rented moving van. While Tina and Edward had been out looking for the money, Mrs. Niles had decided that she could no longer tolerate what she saw as the constant state of crisis engendered by her daughter's residence in the projects. She had decided to mobilize the resources at her command to put a stop to it. She had called a friend of hers whom she knew to have several homes for rent and made arrangements for Tina to move into one of them at her expense.

Several years and many emergencies later, Tina was again ready to move. Since this move was being partially prompted by Tina's dissatisfaction with her landlord, Mrs. Niles suggested that it was about time Tina became her own landlord. Tina's mother once again drew upon her resources to help her daughter. In order to help Tina acquire the house in Roseland, Mrs. Niles used her friends, her knowledge of real estate and banking practices, and her money. The house was being sold by a friend of Mrs. Niles who was moving on to bigger and better things. In order to make sure that Tina's credit rating could bear close scrutiny, her mother transferred a substantial amount of her own cash reserve into Tina's savings account. Mrs. Niles also paid half the down payment and all of the closing costs.

Though she expresses some displeasure that Tina gave up the house, Mrs. Niles also claims that she derives some satisfaction from having taught Tina an object lesson. After being her own landlord for a while, she says, Tina is not always complaining about the inadequacy of landlords. Mrs. Niles says, "She pays the man and keeps her mouth shut." (Mother and daughter exchange smiles without going into exactly how it is she "pays the man.")

What Mrs. Niles emphasizes is that Tina has now reached a point where she is no longer in a state of constant emergency. Nobody has to worry about whether Tina and her children will have enough to eat or whether they will have a roof over their heads. With Tina steadily employed, Mrs. Niles now argues that she can best be of aid to Tina by teaching her how to make her money work for her. She suggests, for example, that Tina should take the portion of her income that she saves by not paying rent and invest it rather than spending it on such items as clothes.

Tina, her sisters, and her daughter all like to dress stylishly. When they do visit with each other, they spend a great deal of time trying on each other's clothes, shoes, wigs, make-up, and jewelry. However, they make no bones about the fact that their mother is the best-dressed woman in the family. The second time that I saw Mrs. Niles she was dressed in winter white from chin to toe. After she had left, I told Tina that her mother had been wearing one of the most stunning outfits I had ever seen. Tina laughed and said, "Girl, you ain't seen nothing. That outfit just matches her white on white deuce and a quarter [Buick Electra 225]." In an only slightly more serious vain Tina explained that her mother was coming from church. "Mother," she said, "goes to church every Sunday, except when she's partied too hard on Saturday night." According to Tina, the snobbish church organization to which her mother belongs wears white once a month. In order to clearly distinguish themselves from the usher board and the missionary society, they insist that the white outfits worn be extremely different from the more pedestrian ones worn by the members of these other organizations.

Tina herself claims that she hasn't been inside of a church since the period in her life after her mother left home and before she married Odie. She points out that even then she was not a regular church member. She belonged instead to a group of popular community singers and went to church only for rehearsals and performances. Tina claims that her appetite for church was ruined when as a little girl she had to attend Apostolic services with her father's mother. She says, "Me and Granny churched all day Sunday, from early in the morning until late at night, and four more nights a week. By the time I was ten years old I had built up enough church credits to last me for the rest of my life."

All the members of the Niles family were born in Chicago. They proudly proclaim their origins to be Northern and urban. Even Edward likes to say that he has never been any further south than the state penitentiary.

The Niles do have relatives who are not considered to be members of the "immediate family." Mrs. Niles has several sisters who live in Chicago. She reports that when their mother was alive and their children were younger, they saw each other and aided each other regu-

larly. Her children know all of their first cousins and remember a time when they saw these relatives every week.
Tina remembers that when her mother's father was alive
he lived with them, while his ex-wife lived with one of
their other daughters. "Once a week, usually on Saturday," she explained, "everybody would come to our
house to see Grandpa. While the grownups talked, the
children would all go out and play. When Grandpa died,
they didn't come nearly so often, but then we would go
and see Grandma once a week, and all the aunts and
cousins would be there." After their mother died, Mrs.
Niles and her sisters drifted apart, seeing each other only
occasionally. The cousins now see each other only once or
twice a year.

In 1979, perhaps partially because there was a researcher asking questions about them, Tina decided that
it was time the kindred came together. She planned a reunion that would coincide with her mother's birthday.
At first she tried to keep the planned affair secret from
her mother, but after talking it over with her aunts she
decided that the proper place to have such an affair was at
her mother's house, and so she had to ask her permission.
For a month, there was much contact with all of these relatives as they planned who would bring what to eat or
drink and solved transportation problems.

When the big day arrived, most of the relatives
came. They ate, drank, reminisced about old times, and
compared presents and futures. In addition to having a
good time, there was much trading of telephone numbers and addresses and many promises to keep in closer
touch and do more things together. Once the big day had
passed, however, there was very little follow-up on these
promises by members of the Niles family.

FIGURE 3.2.

The Niles family, June 1979.

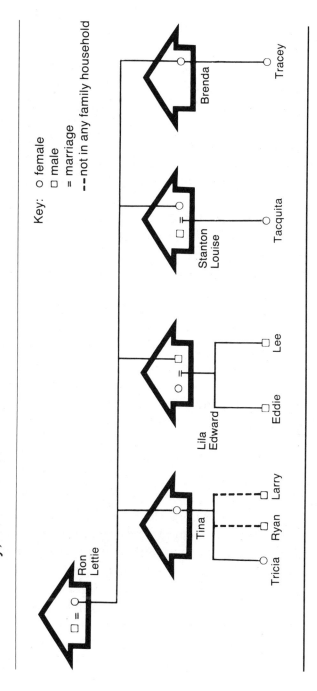

Key: ○ female
      □ male
      = marriage
      -- not in any family household

The information that I was able to gather during the reunion and afterward suggested that two of Mrs. Niles' three sisters were involved in extended families structured much like her own. Each had a husband and three or four adult children. The third sister, a childless widow, was attached to the extended family of the oldest sister. The families exhibited an income range and sources of income much like those of the Niles.

Other relatives were once important to the Niles family but no longer are. Important among these are Mrs. Niles' first husband, the father of all of her children, and his mother. The two younger children lost most meaningful contact with their father when they moved with their mother and her second husband. They have, however, never come to regard their mother's second husband as their father. (The older children love to provoke the normally easygoing Brenda to anger by suggesting that their mother's current husband, Ron, is in fact her biological father.) The reason that Brenda lives apart from her mother is that the relationship between her and her stepfather is such a rocky one.

Edward and his biological father began to have heated arguments as soon as Lettie had moved out of the house. The father, who was then involved in law enforcement, was embarrassed by his son's frequent encounters with the law. One night he declared that if Edward were to get into any more trouble with the law he would disown him. Edward responded by stealing a neighbor's pickup truck and wrecking it on the Dan Ryan expressway. The two have never resolved their differences and assiduously avoid each other's company.

Tina claims that she kept in close contact with her father for quite a while. "Both of us were angry with mother for deserting us.'' Tina says, however, that she soon learned that her father was not dependable. ''I don't think he means any harm, but he is always making promises that he just can't keep. I mean he was always setting me up, promising me that if I did a certain thing he would help me. Then when I'd go to him, he just wouldn't be there. I finally learned that the only one who would back me up was Mother.''

Tina sees the loss of contact with her father's mother in a different light. According to Tina, her Granny has more money than she could spend even if given another whole lifetime. Granny, however, loves her money more than she does people. Tina says, ''Since Daddy is Granny's only child we are the only family she's got. She just doesn't know how to treat people. Once, right after I moved out of the projects, Granny called from Detroit to say she was sick. Her own son wouldn't even go see about her. Mother and her husband went to Detroit and moved her back to Chicago. Mother and Ron even paid for the move. They stored all her furniture at my house and put her in the hospital. Wasn't nothing wrong with her. When she got out of the hospital she came to stay with me. The idea was that she would keep an eye on the children while I was at work. She stayed here for three months. She never watched those kids. She just complained about how much noise they made. She never contributed nothing but complaints about what a sick old lady she was. One day I asked her to loan me $10 to buy something to eat—she was gonna eat too. She claimed she didn't have a penny. The next day I goes in her room to tell her I'm fixing to go out. There she is with a roll big enough to choke a horse. I mean that old lady had $1,200 wrapped up in a greasy paper bag.

"Come to find out that was her income for one month, just one month! I told her that she'd have to pay her own way or move out. Well, do you know that before she would contribute anything on the rent or food she packed up and went back to Detroit. Now she's over there singing that same old song, 'I'm just a little old lady with nobody to look after me.' And everybody is expecting me to take her back in. I wouldn't mind doing nothing for her if she really didn't have no money. But if she wants to hoard her money to herself, then she can just stay by herself."

Summary

IN 1978 and 1979, the organization of the Niles family was extended. The set of intimate kin who participated in a system of mutual aid involving the exchange of goods and services spanned three generations and was spread out over five households.

Residential proximity and involvement in daily exchanges were not requisites for membership in the Niles family. Though each of the five Niles family households was located within the city of Chicago, none of them were located within the same community area nor were they within easy walking distance of each other. Most members of the Niles family did not engage in face to face interaction with each other on a daily basis. Family members did, however, keep in daily contact with each other via the telephone.

The composition of households in the Niles family was stable. The only changes in household composition which took place during the course of the initial study involved adolescent males moving from a family household (the mother's) to a household in another state, which was part of another extended family in which they hold simultaneous membership (the father's).

The Niles family was not economically homogeneous. In fact, what stands out most clearly about the Niles family is that every adult member, but one, had successfully removed themselves from the welfare rolls.

Exchanges between members of the Niles family were predominantly characterized by generalized reciprocity, as indicated by the vagueness of the obligation to return goods and services of commensurate worth in a finite period of time. The generalized nature of the reciprocity within the mutual aid system of the Niles family was emphasized when the parties involved differed in socioeconomic status and one-way flow of goods and services from the haves to the have nots were tolerated over long periods of time.

Exchanges between mobiles in this family appeared to be characterized by balanced reciprocity. Tina and her mother, for example, often loaned each other money expecting payment within a finite period of time. They exchanged gifts on ritual occasions such as birthdays and Christmas with a great deal of time spent making sure that these gifts were equivalent in value.

Before her own mobility was achieved, however, Tina spent many years receiving aid from her mother—aid which she has never been called upon to repay. In the Niles family the emphasis, rather than being on repayment, was on helping family members currently in need. The goods and services that Tina provided for her nonmobile sister were in fact indirect repayment to her mother.

Only Mrs. Lettie Niles found it necessary to isolate

herself from other members of the family in order to be upwardly mobile. Once her mobility was achieved, the isolation was ended. Mrs. Niles then allocated some of the resources made available through her mobility toward helping her children achieve their own mobility.

The one nonmobile member of the Niles family did not find herself isolated from her mobile siblings or her mobile mother. The nonmobile Brenda, because she did not work, was able to visit with other members of the family on a daily basis. Through her visiting patterns, Brenda served as the family's main connector. Brenda also provided the current focus for the mutual aid system of the family. The mobile members of the Niles family perceived Brenda's nonmobile status as a transitory stage in her development as a woman. The cohesiveness of the Niles family was both reflected by and generated through the cooperative efforts of mobile family members to concentrate their resources in such way that Brenda's survival needs were met and the likelihood of her own mobility enhanced.

The Nileses, 1982

SINCE my previous visit, the changes in the Niles family have been primarily developmental. Both Tina and her daughter, Tricia, are now married and living apart from one another. Each of Tina's sisters has given birth to her second child. Louise is still married to and living with Stanton, while Brenda has yet to marry. Tricia is expecting twins, and the members of her family are only slightly shocked that the man she chose to marry is white.

Tina is very proud of her marriage and thinks that it

may just work because her new husband is a hardworking country boy, who even grows vegetables in the backyard of their new home. She half brags and half complains about his extravagance in buying her a brand new Cadillac so that she no longer has to take a cab or the bus home from work at night. She is still working at the telephone company and has been promoted to a position about which she would only laugh and say, "It pays more money than anybody is ever going to make as a teacher. I am quite sure that I bring home your monthly gross every two weeks." She and her husband are discussing the possibilities of going into business. He thinks a tavern or nightclub would be just the kind of endeavor that Tina could manage. He laughs and says, "She has so much experience in them."

Mrs. Niles is still with the same employer and says that though her raises have not really kept up with inflation, she has been able to acquire several additional apartment buildings. She says, "I am not really worried about the state of the Social Security system as long as people have some money left to pay their rent."

Louise has given up her nursing job to start a small catering business. Although she claims the business is easier on her nerves than the hospital was, her family claims that she is trying to work herself to death. Nevertheless, she says, she finally made a small profit last year and that as long as her husband can take care of the household expenses by himself she will continue to work at her business. She says, "You know how nursing is. I can go back whenever I really need to."

Tricia's husband is an elementary school teacher who is trying to convince his wife that once the twins are

FIGURE 3.3.

The Niles family, July 1982.

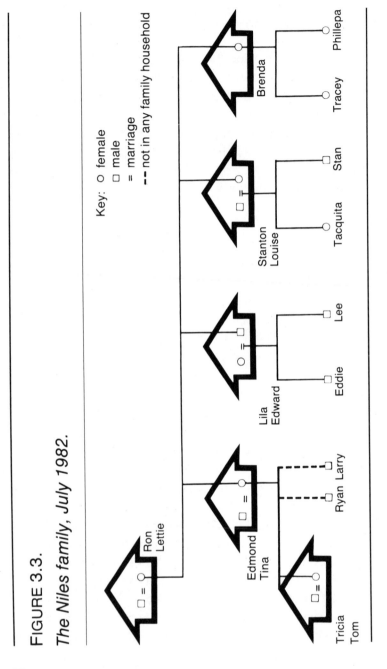

Key: ○ female
      □ male
      = marriage
      -- not in any family household

born and old enough to attend nursery school, she should learn some kind of trade or skill with which to make a living "just in case something were to happen to me."

Tina's brother Edward is still working at the same furniture store. He now thoroughly regrets his youthful prison record, which, he says, has certainly prevented him from reaching his full economic potential. He claims that if his wife were not working they would not be able to make ends meet.

Once again Brenda is the only member of this family who is dependent on welfare payments. Her mother and sisters are at the point of saying, "We give up on that girl. We just give up." They explain their willingness to give up on Brenda in a number of ways. First, she has had a second child (by a different man than her first child!). Second, she refuses her family's offers to pay for schooling, and turned down an offer to work for her sister Louise. Finally, she seems content with her situation. Even with this said, they continue to make sure that she has her rent paid, some food to eat, and clothes for herself and her two children to wear.

The Niles admit that they see even less of each other these days than they did in 1978. Mrs. Niles and Louise claim that they are just too busy working. Tina says that she has been having too much fun playing newlywed to visit relatives. This year the Niles did not even spend the Fourth of July together. Mrs. Niles claimed that it was much too hot to go out in the backyard and that if she started a fire she would barbecue herself. Tina went to Mississippi to meet her in-laws, and Louise catered someone else's holiday celebration. But Brenda and the kids did spend their holiday at Tricia's.

Chapter 4
The Edmondses

ONE of my own cousins, Lloyd, attended Southern Illinois University in Carbondale. There he became a member of a national black Greek letter group. Since he finished school, I have met hundreds of his "brothers." Several of these brothers pass through Lloyd's house every weekend. They socialize, engage in joint business activities, and help each other find places to live and secure employment. It was at Lloyd's that I met Steve Edmonds and convinced him to participate in the research.

I must admit that when I initially interviewed Steve and he spontaneously listed only two relatives, a mother and a brother, I was somewhat dismayed. When I interviewed these two relatives however, I found a set of intimate kin who engaged in mutual aid and spanned five households and four generations.

When I first met Steve, he was working for a local church affiliated community organization. I decided to concentrate on him as the mobile in this family. Soon after the research started, Steve lost his job. It appeared that his mobile status was in doubt. Rather than apply for aid, Steve took an alternative route, which although not as legitimate, was much more lucrative than being on general assistance. For some months, with the knowledge and aid of several members of his family, including his mother, Steve hustled drugs.

Using his unemployment compensation for living expenses, Steve invested his savings in a large quantity of high-quality marijuana. Both his mother and his brother helped him to distribute the smoke by selling nickel ($5) and dime ($10) bags to customers who knocked on their doors. The profits from the marijuana were then reinvested in cocaine which offers a higher profit margin. Steve never stopped looking for a job, and in early June, he was hired by a small, black public relations firm. Steve says the job came just in time, for while he enjoyed the profits in "coke," he had no desire to push his luck and bring himself to the attention of the police.

The drug dealing had also served its purpose. He had paid his mother's taxes and the large heating bill she had accumulated over the past two bad winters. Even more importantly, he had done so without depleting his own financial reserves or having to move in with his mother.

Throughout the initial research period Steve visited a larger proportion of the members of his extended family more often than any of the other mobiles. Four of the five Edmonds family households are located on the same city block, and Steve visited two of these households every day. These visits tended to be of short duration. Steve's mother in fact complained that he didn't really visit with her, but just passed through her house. Steve also talked with the members of his family every day on the phone, and even liked to point out that only the members of his family had both of his telephone numbers. Steve visits his mother more often than he visits any other member of his extended family. To get to his mother's house, Steve must pass his brother's apartment. Sometimes he stops, sometimes he doesn't. Steve argues that his brother, Ed, should have more ambition. Ed's greatest ambition is to keep the job that he has working in a hospital kitchen. He also worries that the Department of Public Aid will discover that he is both married to and living with Karen, who collects an AFDC check for herself and their child.

Steve Edmonds is extremely articulate about why he continues to live in such close proximity to the other members of his extended family. These reasons, in his own terminology, are both "emotional and practical." According to Steve, while he was away at college, he constantly missed the members of his family, especially his mother. When he graduated, he got job offers in New York City and Los Angeles. He turned them down because he wanted to be near his family, at least for a while. He says that while he was in school, he met plenty of people who either had no family or had no sense of family, and he did not want to be like them. These statements take on added significance when consideration is given to the fact that he is also candid about his feelings toward the other members of his family. He says, "I have spent most of my life trying not be like the other members of my family."

At any rate, Steve claims that by the time he was

ready to be separated from them again and was considering job offers from agencies in other cities, his father died
in an automobile accident, and his mother went to
pieces. He says, "after a whole lot of years of a whole lot
of hard times, they were finally getting it together. The
old man had stopped chasing skirts and was working regularly. My brother and I were finally grown up, and then
he died. Mommie was going through the insurance
money like she was going through quarts of vodka. In two
months she had put on fifty pounds and had a shoe box
full of medicine. I stayed here, and sometimes I think I
always will."

Steve Edmonds admits to just "passing through"
his mother's house at least once a day. She, on the other
hand, visits him once a month after giving much advance
notice. Steve's mother, Mommie, says that she would
never dream of showing up at her son's apartment without calling first. His sister-in-law, Karen, says, "Tell the
truth, Mommie. You know that if you did you might not
get in." Karen likes to point out that one of the reasons
Steve passes through so often is to let everyone know that
just because he is at home does not mean that he is available to be visited.

Steve's mother gets the same message across by
hanging hand-lettered DO NOT DISTURB signs over
the door knobs of her front and rear doors. Even her five-
year-old granddaughter knows what these signs mean.
One day the little girl wanted to go to the store with her
father. He said that it was okay, but that she had better
get her mittens and hat. She told him that she had left
them at her grandmother's. He suggested that while he
warmed up the car she should go into her grandmother's
and get them. A few minutes later, she returned to her

FIGURE 4.1.
The Edmonds family, September 1978.

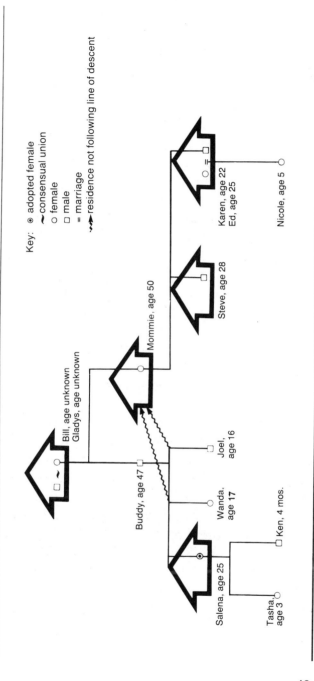

Key: ⊙ adopted female
      ∼ consensual union
      ○ female
      □ male
      = marriage
      ↝ residence not following line of descent

Bill, age unknown
Gladys, age unknown

Mommie, age 50

Buddy, age 47

Joel, age 16

Wanda, age 17

Salena, age 25

Ken, 4 mos.

Tasha, age 3

Steve, age 28

Karen, age 22
Ed, age 25

Nicole, age 5

parents' apartment sobbing loudly. When her mother asked what the problem was, she explained that her father would not let her go with him to the store because she could not get her "stuff" from her grandmother's house. Her mother assumed that the grandmother was not home and told the child to calm down and she would get her keys and open the door for her. The little girl told her "No, Mama. My grandmother is at home, but she has her 'don't bother me' signs up."

When the research began, Steve's mother was not employed outside of the home. Several years ago, her brother Buddy's wife had died following a stroke. Mrs. Edmonds had then taken Buddy's two youngest children into her home to care for them. The children, Joel and Wanda, now sixteen and seventeen years of age, and Mrs. Edmonds were being supported through a combination of government funds and contributions from Buddy.

During the initial research year Mrs. Edmonds acquired a job through the federally funded CETA program. With a title of Geriatric Aide she went to work at a sheltered care home located in a nearby community area. She immediately began to have problems with Joel and Wanda. Both of them began to skip school and to stay out late at night. For several months members of the family argued back and forth about what should be done with them. For a while the family considered making Joel and Wanda more directly accountable to their twenty-five-year-old sister Salena who lived down the street. It was decided, however, that Salena, who suffers from a severely crippling form of arthritis and is separated from her husband, already had her hands full trying to take care of her own two children. In the end it was agreed that the only thing to do with Wanda and Joel was to send them down South to stay with their father and their grandmother. Mrs. Edmonds explained that sending them to Kentucky would provide them with constant supervision by their grandmother, subject them more directly to the authority of their father, and remove them from the greater variety of "bad things to do in Chicago."

On the Saturday morning when their father arrived to pick them up, Joel and Wanda confessed that what they had wanted to do all along was to go to live with him. When all of their requests to do so were denied, they had decided to make such nuisances of themselves that the only viable alternative open to their aunt would be to let them go with their father.

Buddy, who came to Chicago to pick up two children, ended up going home with three. Ed's wife, Karen, had promised Wanda that she would buy her all new underwear, to take to her new home. That Saturday afternoon, as the adults sat around drinking and talking, Wanda constantly reminded Karen of the promise. Finally Karen decided that they would go up to Twenty-Sixth Street and get the underwear, but she conceded that she was too high to walk or to take the bus. She called her grandfather who lives only two blocks away, and he agreed to take them. When her grandfather arrived, Karen decided that she was sober enough to drive. Her grandfather refused to relinquish the steering wheel, and Karen became at first verbally abusive and then struck him in the face with her fist. Mrs. Edmonds, who had been standing on the sidewalk in front of her house giving instructions about what type of underwear should be purchased, grabbed Karen and bodily threw her over the small, white picket fence which separates her front lawn plot from the sidewalk and the street.

A crying Karen got up and went down the street toward her own apartment. Everyone assumed that she had gone to sleep it off and went back to their conversations. Less than half an hour later, Karen's grandfather was back. Rather than going home to sleep, Karen had merely picked up a baseball bat, marched the two blocks to her grandfather's house, and proceeded to break every window she could reach. Not wanting to call the police in on this family matter, her grandfather had come for Ed. Ed talked, pulled, and beat her into his car, and then drove her home, dragged her up the stairs, and put her to bed. A while later Karen's mother showed up crying that Karen had drunk a container of turpentine. Her mother and husband took Karen to the emergency room of a nearby hospital.

In light of these events, the conversation turned to what to do with Karen and Ed's daughter while Karen was in the hospital. Mrs. Edmonds called her mother in Kentucky, whose response to the situation was to say, "Well pack her clothes and bring her too."

Mrs. Edmonds sometimes refers to her apartment as "Grand Central Station." Other times she refers to it as "the supermarket." "My kids (she uses this to mean her children, her grandchild, her nieces and nephew, and her niece's children) don't go to the store to shop. They just shop in my refrigerator and in my pantry." The perhaps not so simple fact of the matter appears to be that the Edmonds organize a great deal of their time around the sharing of food. I had noticed that whenever one member of the family came to visit another, within a few minutes they managed to make it to the kitchen. Once in the kitchen they opened the refrigerator and consumed anything that struck their fancy. Salena claimed that refrigerator peering was the Edmonds family way of saying hello, and one morning she demonstrated to me just how ingrained the practice is.

When I arrived at Salena's that morning she apologized for being unable to offer me anything to eat. She explained that she had been sick and that while her aunt was preparing her meals she simply had not been concerned about going to the grocery store. She pointed out that she was now feeling much better and had asked Ed to take her to the market when he got off from work that afternoon. Anticipating the trip to the grocery store Salena had cleaned her refrigerator leaving nothing in it but a juice jar containing cold water.

While Salena and I were talking Steve came in the back door and headed straight for the refrigerator. A little while later Karen came in to bring home Salena's baby, whom she had kept the night before. She headed straight for the refrigerator. During the next few hours Steve and Karen returned to the empty refrigerator several times. Nobody commented on the condition of the refrigerator until Ed came in. Ed went straight to the box then stood there scratching his head. Finally, he said, "Oh yeah, I'm supposed to take you shopping today." Everybody then began to laugh and to talk about how they had gone back and forth to the refrigerator and were surprised each time to find it empty.

Part of the $180 worth of groceries that Salena purchased that day found their way to Mrs. Edmonds' kitchen. Some went directly there, that is, Salena packed a bag and had Steve take it to his mother. The others arrived by a more circuitous route. A few days later, for example, Salena came into Mrs. Edmonds' house and went straight for the refrigerator. After peering around inside of it for a while she took out two hot dogs and dropped them in a pot. Seeing this, Mrs. Edmonds dropped in the remainder of that package and another entire package.

When the hot dogs were ready it was discovered that Mrs. Edmonds had no bread. Salena then called Wanda and sent her down to her apartment. Her instructions were to ''look in the freezer and you will find four loaves of bread; bring two of them up here.'' After returning with the bread, Wanda discovered that Mrs. Edmonds had no mustard. Several houses had to be searched before the mustard was found. When a jar was finally discovered at Ed and Karen's place, it was the same jar that had been purchased by Salena.

The hot dogs were not the only thing the family shared that day. Salena wanted a joint, and as Steve sat eating his hot dogs, she set out to negotiate a reduced price score from him. She wanted to buy a $5 bag for $3. Mrs. Edmonds joined in the negotiations, pointing out that everyone would like a joint, some beer, and some fish. She then went through the house collecting from each adult. Within fifteen minutes, Salena's initial $3 had been joined by cash contributions sufficient to buy a dime bag, a case of beer, and enough fish to feed the entire family. Mrs. Edmonds then added enough to buy greens and a pint of vodka (reminding everyone that she neither smokes marijuana nor drinks beer).

While Steve and Ed went to do the shopping, the women sat around the kitchen table and talked; they talked about their neighbors, their children, and their loves. When the men came back they joined in the conversation, which toned down some in their presence. The women picked the greens, Mrs. Edmonds cooked, and everybody smoked and drank. When the food was done, the small children were fed first, their mothers cutting up their greens and picking the bones out of their fish. Teenagers and adults fixed their own plates from the stove. When the meal was over they all sat around the kitchen for a while. Then, as tiny heads began to nod off to sleep, the family members dispersed to their own households saying "See you tomorrow."

The other members of the Edmonds family, even if somewhat reluctantly, admit looking up to Steve. They variously praise him for having either "common sense" or "street sense" to go along with his "book sense." Each member of the family admits that in some way or another they are indebted to Steve. Salena says, "It may sound strange, him being a man and all, but Steve's the one who can always tell when something is wrong with me and then tries to do something about it. If I'm broke, he'll let me have money. I've been owing him a hundred dollars for years. Every time I give him something on it, I have to go back and get it again. If I'm depressed, he'll try to do something about that too. Sometimes he just comes and talks to me and sometimes he just listens. Sometimes he just plays with the kids."

Even the kids are very up on Steve. Salena's baby, whom members of the family call "Froggy," breaks into giggles every time Steve appears. He then throws his arms up in the air in anticipation of being picked up and thrown into the air, then caught and cuddled. The other children contend over this attention and affection. One day Salena's three-year-old daughter, Tasha, seeing Steve enter the room, bounded out of her chair and ran

FIGURE 4.2.
The Edmonds family, June 1979.

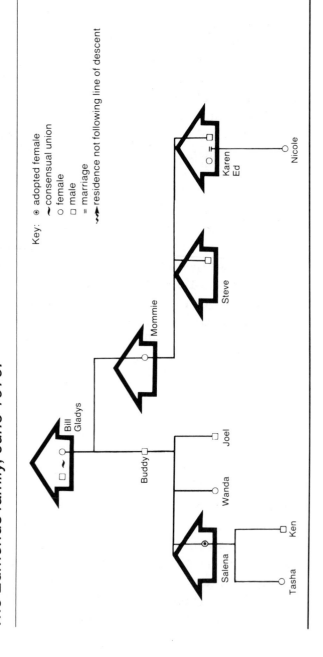

Key:
⊙ adopted female
〜 consensual union
○ female
□ male
= marriage
➤ residence not following line of descent

Bill
Gladys

Mommie

Karen
Ed

Nicole

Steve

Buddy

Joel

Wanda

Salena

Tasha   Ken

toward him saying, "Hi, Uncle Steve." Before she made it to him, however, she was intercepted by Ed and Karen's five-year-old Nicole, who loudly announced, "He is not your uncle, he is just your cousin." It was quite obvious that for Nicole this meant she had first right to a hug from Steve and the only right to sit on his knee. When Steve sat down Nicole hopped up and pushed Tasha back every time she tried to get close. When Steve explained that Tasha had just as much right to a knee as she did and that if she wanted to sit on one knee Tasha would be allowed the other, Nicole stormed out of the room. A well-satisfied Tasha enjoyed the lap alone for about five minutes, after which a contrite Nicole reappeared and said, "Okay, Steve. I'll share."

Mrs. Edmonds, however, is the biggest Steve booster. According to her, Steve is the best son that any mother could ask for. Though she admits that he is sometimes too bossy, acting like he was the parent and she the child, he always comes through when she needs him. The only thing he could do which would make her happier would be to marry and produce for her some additional grandchildren. She hopes that her new employment will make him feel free to do so.

Whenever his mother becomes vocal in that direction, Steve becomes visibly agitated. According to him the biggest problem that blacks face in adapting to modern society is their propensity for producing children that they have no means of supporting. He insists that he will neither marry nor produce children until he can provide some degree of security for his spouse and their offspring. And that, he says, will take a lot more effort than the things he does for the members of his extended family. "I don't do anything for them that they wouldn't do for me if the situation was different. After all, we are a family.''

Though Mrs. Edmonds admits to being born in rural Arkansas, she claims that her early move to Chicago wiped out any Southern rural heritage. According to Mrs. Edmonds, her mother was an only child who moved to Chicago as a young woman. Two years later, when she had married and settled down, her parents followed bringing Mrs. Edmonds, who was then five years old. They left no family in Arkansas and never returned there. She points out that though her mother and brother now live in the South, they do not live in the state from which her mother originally came. Mrs. Edmonds explains that it was in the mid 1960s that her stepfather decided to move back to Kentucky to personally oversee some land and a small grocery store which had been left to him by a relative. He took his wife with him. After his death she stayed on because running the small store allows her to be financially independent. Mrs. Edmonds' mother is the only member of the family who attends church regularly, and even she mixes her Methodist religion with strong doses of homespun wisdom (to explain, for example, why she has a live-in boyfriend some years her junior and large quantities of scotch).

After I had been observing the Edmonds family for some time, I noticed that when Salena used the term ''father'' she did not always appear to be referring to Buddy Edmonds. In an attempt to understand, I collected a spontaneous listing and a genealogy from her. I discovered that Salena was five years old at the time her mother left her father and married Buddy Edmonds. Because Salena's mother severed ties not only with her ex-husband and his family, but with her own family as well, the Edmonds family was the only family Salena knew as she was growing up. Salena says it never occurred to her to contact any of her other relatives until she herself was married and expecting her first child. Getting in touch with them was easier than she thought it would be though much less rewarding. Since both her maternal and paternal grandparents still live in the small Mississippi town where her parents were born, she received replies to letters addressed to them in care of general delivery in that town. Both of the replies were warm and supplied her with her father's address and telephone number in New York City. She laughs at how excited she was when she got the letters and how she had showed them to Ed that night when he came to her apartment. Ed, she says, was aghast because no one had ever told him that they were not blood relatives. Ed even admits that he did not calm down until he broached the subject with his mother and she calmly asked, "Well, at this late date, does it really make any difference?" Ed had to admit that it didn't.

Salena said she had really been hoping her father would be overjoyed to hear from his long lost daughter. Instead, when she called, he sounded rather put out and told her that if she were looking for money she had come to the wrong place. He told her that he had always known where she was, but had never bothered to contact her because he wasn't all that certain that she was his daughter. He told her that her mother had been a tramp and that she was probably one too. Salena says that first conversation was enough for her, and she never tried to contact him again, though she does hear about him from her grandparents with whom she is in regular though not frequent contact. While it is tempting to see Salena's inclusion in the Edmonds family as an example of fictive kinship, it appears most properly treated as an example of adoption, however informal.

In a family where the pooling of food is so apparent and where the exchanges of other goods and services are predominantly characterized by generalized reciprocity, the behavior of one member, Ed, and the family's reaction to it stand out. On the Sunday afternoon when Buddy was getting ready to go back to Kentucky, for example, he and Ed had been sitting in one corner of the living room talking for several hours. The conversation had veered from cars to women and back again to cars. Ed was trying to talk his uncle into letting him have some tires for considerably less than Buddy was willing to sell them for. Finally, Buddy looked around and addressed his comment to the whole assemblage. ''What,'' he said, ''have ya'll been feeding this boy? He is truly crazy.'' Ed responded before anyone else could, ''I don't know why I'm always trying to get something for nothing from my own family.'' As the members of the family laughed, Steve came in with, ''Because, just like the man said, boy, you are truly crazy.''

Summary

THE set of intimate kin who participated in this family's system of mutual aid spanned four generations and five households. Residential proximity and involvement in daily exchanges were not requisites for membership in the Edmonds family. Though four of the Edmonds family households were located on the same block of Chicago's Lawndale community, the fifth was located in a different state. While those members of the family who lived in close proximity to each other visited with each other daily, even taking most of their meals together, interaction and exchanges with geographically distant family members took place less often and primarily via the telephone.

The composition of the Edmonds family households was stable. The only changes in household composition which took place during the course of the study involved two adolescents moving from a family household located in Chicago to a family household located in Kentucky.

The Edmonds family was economically heterogeneous. Over the course of the study we were able not only to observe that members of the Edmonds family had experienced mobility at different paces, but also to observe individuals in the process of change from one status to another.

Exchanges between members of the Edmonds family were predominantly characterized by generalized reciprocity as indicated through the vagueness of the obligation to return goods and services of commensurate worth within a finite period of time. As was the case with the Niles family, when the parties to the exchange differ in socioeconomic status the generalized nature of the reciprocity became even more apparent as there was a great tolerance of one-way flows from the haves to the have nots.

One way in which the Edmonds family differed from the Niles family was that in the Edmonds family the ratio of haves to have nots was much smaller. This means that it was much more difficult for members of the Edmonds family to concentrate their resources on either the survival or the mobility of a single member. Members of the Edmonds family, when compared to members of the

Niles family, had also experienced a higher rate of fluctuation in the status of individual family members. Comparing the two families suggests that a higher rate of fluctuation in the status of individual family members results in a decrease in the length of time over which imbalances in the flow of goods and services can be allowed to exist without resulting in the disruption of the family. The hostilities, conflicts, and subsequent family disruption which might result from this smaller ratio of mobiles and the higher rate of economic instability, however, is mediated through the utilization of "pooling" as a redistributive mechanism.

In the Edmonds family, goods and services were concentrated on the person and in the household of Mrs. Mommie Edmonds. All family members, not just mobiles, made contributions to her, although mobiles were the only ones who made cash contributions on a regular basis. This was done with the knowledge that her storehouse can be drawn upon whenever one was in need.

Mrs. Edmonds received goods from all directions and redistributed them in all directions, making sure that at any point in time, the main direction of the flow was from the haves to the have nots. Even when she was dependent on welfare herself, Mrs. Edmonds would often take the cash contributions of mobiles and immediately transfer all or part of them to family members in need. Her actions greatly reduced the potential for conflict between mobile and nonmobile family members, for the nonmobile member who ended up with the contribution was then explicitly indebted to Mrs. Edmonds rather than to the mobile.

Though differences in socioeconomic status were potentially disruptive, the pooling mechanism served to foster family cohesion. All members of the family understood that if and when they needed help, they could depend on their family to make sure that their needs for survival were met.

The Edmondses, 1982

A CURSORY glance at the diagrams might lead one to think that of the three families I was able to locate, the Edmonds family has changed least of all. The diagram shows only the birth of Ed and Karen's new baby and that Salena has reconciled with her husband. In this case, however, the diagrams are slightly misleading.

Salena's reconciliation with her husband has meant a move to the other side of town and a greater degree of isolation from the other members of her family. According to Salena, the only member of her family that her husband really cares for is Steve. Salena says that when other members of her family come to visit her, her husband is quite rude to them. He also gets upset if she goes to visit them very often. "My aunt," she says "understands that this is the way things have to be, because he is taking care of me. He is doing the things that they used to do for me. I mean she couldn't help me so much with Ed and Karen both not working and them having the new baby and all. Not seeing each other so much is the price we have to pay for me now being able to help her out some time."

Salena explains that, because her husband now has a steady and relatively high paying job, she is now able to sneak cash contributions to her aunt. She has to sneak them because her husband knows that they would be used to help Karen and Ed, whom he really dislikes and considers to be "lazy, alcoholic dopeheads." She makes these contributions behind her husband's back because "Well, my aunt was there when I really needed somebody and where was he? I still don't know that he won't take off again, but, well, my family will always be there to do whatever they can."

Salena further admits that when she and her husband first moved she talked to her aunt on the phone every day and still made a point of seeing her at least once a week. After a year, however, she points out that she only talks to her aunt about once a week and sees her only about once a month. Salena's husband is currently under consideration for a promotion, which would require them to move to the West Coast. I cannot help but wonder if such a move would result in her being almost totally isolated from the family that she once spent all of her time with.

Salena, however, is not the only member of the Edmonds family whose connections have changed. Steve has also removed himself from close residential proximity to his family and reduced the frequency with which he interacts with them. While these things by themselves might mean nothing, there has also been a change in his attitude. He still talks with his mother every day and continues to make cash contributions to her. ("Not as much as I used to though. I mean the rent on this apartment is really killing me.") When I asked Steve if his move had anything to do with the fact that both Ed and Karen were unemployed and living off of his mother, his only response was, "Well I don't want to say anything negative about my family. So I would really rather not talk about it."

My conversation with Steve led me to believe that

FIGURE 4.3.
The Edmonds family, July 1982.

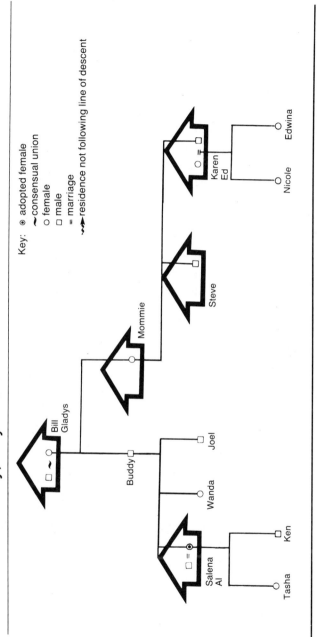

Key: ⊙ adopted female
     ⌒ consensual union
     ○ female
     □ male
     = marriage
     ➤ residence not following line of descent

Bill
Gladys

Mommie

Buddy

Steve

Karen
Ed

Salena
Al

Wanda

Joel

Nicole

Edwina

Tasha

Ken

since my previous visit, the Edmonds family had reached some kind of breaking point when Ed lost his job, a point at which there were simply too many have nots and two few haves. Whether Steve wants to admit it or not, his move seemed to be a way of limiting his obligation to the other members of the family so that he could have more of his resources for his own goals in life.

Salena on the other hand seems to be implying that when things got really rough for Ed and Karen, she and her children were not getting as much help as before. She then took advantage of the only opportunity open to her to become a have rather than a have not.

Back in Lawndale, where Mrs. Edmonds and Ed and Karen continue to live, things go on as usual. They still eat together, and when Mrs. Edmonds is not at work they can often be found drinking together. When Mrs. Edmonds' mother, Buddy, Wanda, and Joel came for the Fourth of July, even Steve and Salena were there.

Chapter 5
The Bakers

BETTY Adams Wynne, who has been a close friend of mine since childhood, is a beautician. Rather than working in a salon, Betty fixes hair in the kitchen of her apartment. Her customers include members of her family, her husband's family, their other relatives, neighbors, and friends, and the wives of the men with whom her husband works. Knowing the type of informant I was looking for, Betty approached her customers, asking if any of them knew of a young, single black male who had been raised on welfare and who would be interested in participating in my research. Ann Baker Victor, a customer whose husband works with Betty's husband, suggested that her nephew Marcus might be interested and offered to introduce me to him.

When I was first introduced to Marcus Baker, he was a twenty-year-old unemployed high-school dropout. Marcus lived in a female headed household which was located in a public housing project, supported by welfare payments, and already into the third generation. To identify the residents of this household as Marcus' family, however, would be to leave out many of his socially significant kin.

Interviewing Marcus, his mother, and his grandmother, I discovered a set of intimate relatives. After observing the interactions between and among these relatives, I was able to isolate those who engaged in a system of mutual aid with each other. The Baker family, so defined and identified, is spread out over seven households (six located in Chicago and one in Milwaukee) and four generations. The only changes in the composition of these households over the initial study period involved Marcus joining the army and one of his sisters giving birth to a child.

Ann Baker Victor, the woman I met at the beauty parlor, is the mobile Baker on whom I concentrated. Ann is married, and her husband's income contributes significantly to her level of living. Ann, however, is employed and meets the criteria for mobile status on her own. Ann lives farther away from any kin than the other mobiles. She has no family members living next door to her or down the street from her, and doesn't even have kin living in contiguous community areas. Ann insists that it is this geographical separation which prevents her from seeing the members of her family more often than once a week. It does not keep her from talking to them on the phone several times a day.

Residential proximity, however, is only one dimension of physical accessibility. Ann, in fact, has one major complaint about her job. She must work on weekends and misses the congregation of her sisters at their mother's house on Saturday and Sunday. One Sunday while I was at her mother's house Ann called no fewer than five times. She was constantly checking to see which family members had arrived, which ones had left, and just what was going on. She spoke, at least briefly, to everyone present that day (about twenty-five people over the course of the day). She even spoke to me saying, "You guys sound like you are having a great ole time."

When I asked Ann why she lived so far from all the members of her family, she was insistent about pointing out that they were the ones who had created the residential separation. She says that from the time the family moved to Chicago from Chicago Heights in 1950 until about eight years ago, all of her sisters except Dean lived on the West Side. "Dean moved to Milwaukee with J.D. when all the rest of us were still living at home with Mama. When the rest of them started moving out, they never moved very far from Mama, and every time that Mama moved, they moved. When Mama finally moved to the South Side, they moved to the South Side, too. Jean and Maxie looked like they was having a contest to see which one of them could move the farthest south. As for me, I don't like the South Side. I'm a West Side girl, and I guess I always will be. It's just me and Sharon left west now."

Further questioning revealed that Ann's husband, Tom, absolutely refuses to consider moving south. He works in a northwestern suburb and claims that he can see no reason to move further away from his job. He and Ann are now in the process of looking for a house to buy. Tom assured me that it would not be any farther from his place of employment.

Ann visits her mother's household more often than

she visits the household of any other extended family member. The household she visits next often is that of her sister Sharon, who is only ten months older than she is. Ann lives closer to her mother and Sharon than to any other members of the family. While their mother has been supported by welfare for most of her adult life, Sharon, like Ann, has been mobile.

When asked why she doesn't visit her other sisters more often, Ann generally offers an explanation that relies on the distance they live from each other, and points out that she used to visit them more often when they lived closer together. She points out, for example, that when she got her first apartment it was right across the street from where Jean was living, and she visited with her every day.

Jean, the sister who is most dissimilar to Ann in socioeconomic status, offers a counterexplanation for why her sisters and even her mother do not visit her that often. According to Jean's reasoning, it can't be a simple matter of distance. She explains that everybody visits Maxie more often than they do her, yet she and Maxie live fewer than ten minutes apart by car. In Jean's view, the members of her extended family don't visit her more often because they have an impression of the housing project in which she lives as a dangerous place to be. She claims that this impression is erroneous.

Jean may find some comfort in the fact that there is one sister whom Ann never visits. Surprisingly enough this is not the sister who lives in Milwaukee, for Ann manages to visit Dean there at least three times a year. The sister that Ann *never* visits (and the emphasis is Ann's) is Christine. When asked why she never visits Christine, Ann says simply, "Well, I have never been one of Christine's favorite people."

Correspondingly, Christine never visits Ann. Well, almost never. In 1979 Ann and her husband, Tom, decided that they would really throw themselves a big bash for their tenth wedding anniversary in May. The guest list was made up mainly of the members of their extended families, including Christine. Ann said, "Well, you know I see her every week at Mama's house, so inviting her was no problem. I don't really expect her to come." On the night of the party Ann had gone into the bathroom when Christine came through the front door with Eve and Eve's date, Luther. The members of the family who saw Christine stopped talking, stopped drinking, and waited expectantly. When Ann came out of the bathroom and saw Christine, she yelled, lay down on the floor, and rolled around (in her new white dress). The family clapped and whistled as Ann got up and embraced Christine.

Even Christine's showing up at the party and Ann's hearty welcome did not seem to signify a great change in their relationship. They never got close to each other or engaged in conversation for the rest of the evening. They will probably continue to see each other primarily "at Mama's house."

Ann visits her mother at least once a week. Her mother visits her "about three times a year, if I can make it a special occasion, make sure that she has a way to get here and that she has a way back home." (Even with these special arrangements made, Ann was worried that her mother would not show up for the anniversary party. Her mother assured her that she would put in a brief appearance and she did.)

I was able to talk to Amy Baker, Ann's mother, at length about why she doesn't visit more often. According to Amy, her daughters get very jealous of one another,

FIGURE 5.1.

The Baker family, September 1978.

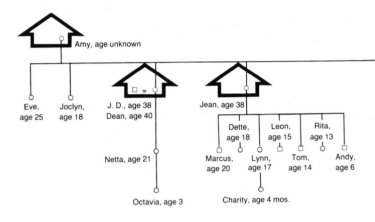

and if she visits one she has to visit them all, unless she can justify the visit as having occurred for a special reason. From September to May she had made only five visits. She went to Maxie's house for Marcus's going away party. She went to Jean's to see her new "greatgrand." She went to see an ill Christine, she went to Ann's for the anniversary party, and she went with Ann and Sharon to visit Dean in Milwaukee on Mother's Day. Amy says, "If

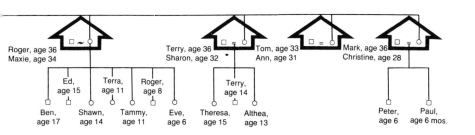

Key: ~ consensual union
     O female
     □ male
     = marriage
     -- not in any family household

I visited as much as they want me to, I wouldn't never be at my own house. And besides, young people don't really be wanting old folks around. We cramps they style and then they say we be meddling. I'm they Mama and if they wants to see me, they will just have to come to me.''

I have mentioned that the Bakers congregate at Amy's almost every weekend. They also spend a great deal of time visiting each other independently and debat-

ing about whose turn it is to visit whom. One Sunday I
rode with Ann to her mother's house. When we arrived,
Sharon and her children along with the family members
normally resident in Amy's household were already
there. Only a short while after we arrived Maxie's eldest
son, Ben, came in. He had driven his mother's car to work
that day and had stopped by to see if there was anything
his grandmother needed or wanted him to do for her. He
stayed long enough to enjoy some of the oxtail stew she
had fixed for dinner and left with instructions to take the
car directly home to his mother so that she could come
over.

Several hours later Ben still had not made it home,
and his mother was getting very distressed over the idea
that she might miss visiting with her mother and sisters.
She and Ann carried on a series of negotiations over the
telephone until Ann agreed to go and pick her up. Just as
the two of them made it back to Amy's house, Jean was
on the phone. She wanted everyone to know that she was
hurt that arrangements would be made to pick up Maxie
while she was left "stuck in this house with these crazy
children." Ann got on the phone and pointed out that
she was the one who had gone to get Maxie. She explained that she had done so because Maxie often comes a
very long distance to visit her and was willing to let the
trip from their mother's house and back count as a full
visit from Ann. Jean countered with the idea that she
would come and visit Ann more often if she had a car and
that if she did have a car and Ann was without one she
would come and visit Ann without demanding a return
visit.

They spent the better part of the afternoon "debat-

ing" about who owed whom a visit and whether the circumstances permitted them to "pay up." Though the issue was never really resolved, it did serve to point out that
those Bakers who don't visit each other often felt a need
to explain that behavior to an outsider, to the rest of the
family, and to each other.

The next week, Ann called me up to report that Jean
had been over to her house. Jean was in the process of becoming an Eastern Star and needed a long white dress.
After shopping for something appropriate, she decided
that it would be better to get someone to make the dress
for her. That someone was Ann. Ann wondered aloud
why Jean had not asked Christine, who is the best seam-
stress in the family. She knew of course, as I did, that
Jean's relationship with Christine was worse than her
own.

Ann reminded me of the controversy that had arisen
on the past weekend and pointed out that "Jean can find
her way over here when she wants something." From the
dress episode to the end of the study period, however,
Ann made several trips to Jean's: once to take Jean's
daughter to the hospital, once to take Amy to see the new
baby, and once merely to visit Jean.

The normal visiting patterns of the Bakers with each
other can be fairly simply, if here crudely, presented.
Amy Baker receives regular visits from each of her daughters, even the daughter who lives in Milwaukee. Dean in
fact visited her mother more often than she realized.
When I first interviewed her, she estimated that she came
to see her mother an average of six or seven times a year. It
would now appear more accurate to say that in the twenty
years she has lived in Milwaukee she has never come fewer

than six times a year. The average, however, is closer to nine times a year. In the first five calendar months of 1979 she had already made five visits.

Though several of her sisters visit her in Milwaukee during the year, when she comes to Chicago, Dean goes to their homes only for special occasions, such as Marcus' going-away party and Ann's anniversary party. The rest of the time she does what I can only describe as "hold court" at her mother's house. Her sisters refer to Dean as the "Big Apple." Dean says she wishes that they would leave the adjective off. Her sisters however are not referring to the fact that she is overweight or to the fact that she is the "best off" family member. The term is used rather to imply that she is a very special person to them.

In many small ways, they treat Dean as they treat their mother. They follow her around the house talking to her and then complain what a hard job it is because she, like their mother, is always moving. When she finally does sit down, they vie for a place next to her. I have seen Ann pay one of her nieces fifty cents to hold her place near Dean while she went to the bathroom. The enterprising niece auctioned the place off and ended up with two dollars. While this was going on, all the members of the family who were present were laughing and screaming with the sheer fun of it, and Dean was basking in it.

Dean's own daughter Netta says, "I don't know why you guys make such a fuss over her. When I get back home, she won't know how to act." As the oldest grandchild, however, she enjoys the same sort of popularity among her cousins. When they find out she is in town, it is almost impossible to keep them from coming to see her. Her own daughter, Octavia, is the oldest "greatgrand," and already the "Big Apple" moniker is sometimes applied to her.

Jean visits her mother regularly, though, she insists, not as often as she did before she moved so far away, became a grandmother, wrecked her car, ad infinitum. The family member Jean visits with next regularly is her sister Maxie. The frequency with which Maxie reciprocates is always the subject of some controversy. Jean says, "When I had my car, I used to go over to Maxie's every day. We would go shopping or wherever we felt like going. Now that she's got a car and I don't, well she forgets about me." The very next day Maxie and Jean went shopping together. They had gone to a wholesale house where they bought candy to sell to the children in their neighborhoods. Both reported that the venture was a failure because their own children ate up the profits. I have often tried to reach Maxie by phone only to discover that she was not home. When her children had grown used enough to me to report her whereabouts their most frequent answer was "over at Jean's."

Maxie also visits Ann with some regularity. She says Ann's house is a place where she can relax her nerves because there are no children in it and most people never think to look for her there. Ann, however, visits with and is most regularly visited by her sister Sharon. Ann makes a very telling comment about her relationship with Sharon. According to Ann, Sharon's oldest daughter, Theresa, wishes that she had the same type of relationship with her own sister. What Theresa doesn't understand, Ann says, is that "Sharon and I aren't just sisters, we are friends."

Even the supposedly antisocial Christine visits her mother's house, not just to see her mother, but also to visit her sister Eve. Eve in turn goes to visit her. At the beginning of the study period Jean and Maxie pointed out that they did not even have Christine's address. When they would ask her where she lived she would simply say, "Down the street from where I used to live." It took the ever devious Maxie to find out exactly where that was. While talking to her mother one day, Maxie learned that Christine was ill. Maxie convinced her mother that if she were in fact a dutiful mother she would go and visit her sick daughter, and volunteered to drive her. Having learned through her own resourcefulness where Christine lived, Maxie exclaimed, "Girl, you ain't never gonna be smart enough to put one over on your big sister." With only mild protests from Christine, Maxie packed up her children and took them home with her. She kept them until Christine was feeling better.

Ann not only visits with the members of her extended family, she also participates in their system of mutual aid. Both the Baker family system of mutual aid and Ann's involvement in it deserve further description. Ann involves herself in her family's system of mutual aid by making regular cash contributions to her mother, by giving or loaning money to her less-well-off sisters (especially for things needed by their children), by providing emergency services, and by engaging in ritualized exchanges with sisters not needing financial assistance.

According to Amy Baker, Ann has had some type of independently earned income since she was fourteen years old. Whenever it has been possible Ann has shared her pay with her mother. Ann and Amy now like to tell this story to indicate how ingrained the practice is. When Ann and Tom planned their anniversary party they agreed that Ann would pay for all of the food while Tom bought all of the liquor. The day they finally made it to the grocery store, however, Ann came home sad because she had spent her entire paycheck. Tom got on the phone and called Amy. He told her that her daughter was about to cry, and he didn't want that to happen because the entire purpose behind the party was to make her happy. Amy advised that Tom could always make Ann happy by greasing her palm. With that advice in mind, Tom told Ann that if she would not cry, he would give her $200. As soon as Tom had gone to work Ann called Amy and explained that now that Tom was going to make up for some of what she had spent on the party, Amy could expect to receive her regular contribution.

Three of the eight Baker sisters (Jean, Maxie, and Sharon) never graduated from high school. Each of them regrets the fact and tries to encourage her own children not to repeat the same mistake. Dean's daughter Netta managed to graduate even though she was pregnant at the time (replicating her mother's behavior). Jean has been sorely disappointed that each of her older children dropped out. As Maxie's oldest son, Ben, approached his graduation, the entire family became anxious for him—afraid that something would go wrong. His mother was especially concerned that if he were not able to participate in all the pomp and circumstance surrounding the occasion he would not go through with it. Ann offered her help. She talked to Ben often about the advantage of graduating, paid for his class ring, his senior pictures, and his cap and gown.

Ann did not see this as unusual behavior as it was exactly what Dean had done for her a long time ago. She also pointed out that she had been helping to pay nominal school fees for Jean's children for several years. The practice started with Jean borrowing the money but never being able to pay it back. Because Ann did not want the children to suffer, she simply went ahead and made the payments as gifts to them.

The type of emergency service Ann is willing to provide can be seen in the circumstances surrounding the birth of WeeWee. On December 28, 1978, Marcus's mother Jean decided to go out for the evening. While she was out her daughter Dette went into labor. At first Dette wasn't sure that her pains indicated that birth was close at hand. Her sister Lynn came in, however, and with her previous experience in childbirth assured Dette that it was "the real thing." Dette then called her grandmother Amy to find out if she knew where Jean could be reached. Amy didn't know where Jean was, but after timing the contractions with her granddaughters over the phone suggested that they had better find someone to take Dette to the hospital. Dette then called her Aunt Maxie, who rushed out of the house only to discover that her car would not start. Maxie then called Ann, who picked up Maxine, and together they went to pick up Dette and take her to the hospital.

I heard this story several times, from its participants and from those who were not actually involved (the new baby's six-year-old uncle told it to me twice). Considering the distance involved, I questioned Ann at some length about why, after working a split shift as a directory assistance operator for Illinois Bell, finally making it home on a cold winter night at 11 P.M., eating her dinner, taking her bath, and going to bed, she would then get up and drive all the way across town to take someone to the hospital. Her answers to my questions made it quite clear that the trip would not have been made for just anyone. This trip was made because it involved a niece and an as yet unborn kinsperson. Ann said, "I really didn't have any choice. I never thought about not going. I thought about waiting for my husband to get home from work so that he could go with me. But I was scared that would be too late. If anything happened to Dette or that baby because I didn't go, well, how would I ever be able to live with myself?"

Some of the things that Ann does for members of her family have a quality which is more ritually than practically necessitated. Every newborn baby, for example, gets a hand-crocheted gift from Auntie Ann. Ann gets incensed when mere friends expect her to spend that much of her time and energy making sweater or carriage sets for children born into their families. For people outside of the family, she says, "I would just rather go and buy them something." The larger children never know when they might get a gift from Auntie Ann. ("I saw this in the store and it reminded me so much of you that I just had to buy it for you.") They do know that reports of good behavior by their parents and good report cards from school carry more weight than simple requests from them.

Ann says that it sometimes seems that family members expect more from her because she doesn't have any children of her own. But she also says that they know that she is going to do only what she wants to do, and they don't spend time trying to pressure her.

Ann's behavior is not remarkably different from that of her other mobile sisters. Dean and Sharon both make regular cash contributions to their mother. They all

FIGURE 5.2.

The Baker family, June 1979.

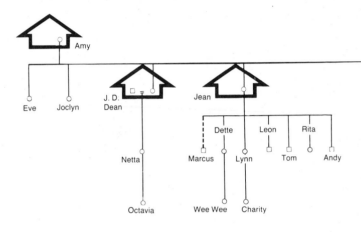

know that Amy disposes of this income as she sees fit and that often means redistributing it to her less well-off daughters.

The less well-off daughters also try to give to Amy. One of Maxie's attempts at giving shows this and sheds light on how it is that members of extended families come to learn that sharing is proper behavior. One Sunday, when I was visiting Amy Baker, Maxie called. She

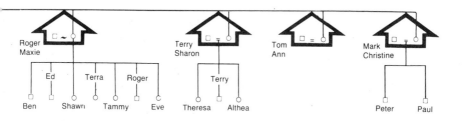

Key: ~ consensual union
      ○ female
      □ male
      = marriage
      -- not in any family household

was so upset by the behavior of her youngest son, Roger, that she had to call and share it with her mother and the other members of her family who were at her mother's house.

Maxie, it seems, had been getting ready to come over to her mother's house. As she was putting the leftovers from her Sunday dinner into the refrigerator, Maxie decided that she would take her mother some of the meat

which was crowding her upright freezer to the point that
she had to lean on it to get it closed. She got a shopping
bag down and was loading it up when little Roger came
into the kitchen and said: "Ain't you glad my Daddy
ain't here so you can take that meat to Grandma?"

"Imagine," Maxie says, "that little sucker talking
to me like I could steal something out of my own house. I
told him, 'Boy, I don't care who here and who ain't. I
take anything I want to my Mama anytime I want to.' "

By the time Maxie and her children made it to
Amy's house, everyone had heard the story. She still had
to repeat it for the entire group—and by that time it had
even acquired a name, "Roger and the Meat." Everytime
the story was told, the adults in the family would laugh
uproariously and the other children would tease a blush-
ing Roger unmercifully. The ridicule to which Roger
found himself subjected reached a high point when late
in the evening he announced that he was hungry and his
grandmother took him into the kitchen and fixed him a
heaping plate of food.

The Baker sisters generally eat and feed their men
and children before coming to their mother's house.
Once there they eat again. The meal is so small, however,
that it can only be seen as a ritual. They compete for very
small tastes of Amy's food and then declare that nobody
can cook as good as Mama. Amy smiles and says how good
it is to have them come over and eat because the children
she has left at home don't appreciate good cooking.

Several events further highlight the nature of the relationship among members of the family. One of these is
called "Our Trip to Las Vegas." After the snowiest winter in Chicago's history, Ann and Sharon decided that a
trip to Las Vegas would make everyone feel better. They

looked into the necessary arrangements and told everyone how much money the trip would require. Ann, Sharon, and Dean had no trouble getting money together and offered to pay their mother's way. Amy declined saying, "If God had wanted people to fly, he would have given them wings." Eve stepped in quickly and explained that she really wanted to go even though she was temporarily short of funds. The three well-off sisters conferred. They decided that an offer to pay Eve's way would fly in the face of Jean and Maxie, who, though they offered other rationalizations, simply could not afford to go. Eve pointed out that if she could borrow the cost of the packaged airfare and hotel accommodations, she had her own spending money. The four of them agreed that each of the three well-off sisters would loan Eve one-third of the amount she needed. Eve has never paid any of this money back. The amount owed has become a permanent debt in light of which all future applications for money will be reviewed.

Jean and Maxie found themselves in a similar situation. They were already so deeply in debt to their better-off sisters that they could not bring themselves to borrow money for a pleasure trip. Finally, Jean said plainly that she could not afford to go and involved herself no farther in the trip. Maxie, although she could not go, participated in the trip vicariously. She showed up for each of the planning sessions and as her sisters gushed about what a good time they were going to have in Las Vegas, she pronounced, with her usual candor, "You just don't know how much I hate you hot-shot bitches." When their plane finally took off from O'Hare, Maxie was standing among their husbands unabashedly crying.

All the while they were enjoying the champagne

flight and the adult amusement park atmosphere of Vegas, the four Baker sisters were never able to completely remove Maxie's tearful face from their minds. They sent her many postcards and brought her back gifts. When their plane brought them back to Chicago, Maxie was at the airport waiting for them, still verbalizing her envy, but without rancor.

It had been brought to my attention that I had never offered precise criteria for deciding whether or not some relative was really in or out of the family. Admittedly, my criteria are somewhat like the beast I study; in the immortal words of Charles H. Johnson, ''amorphous.'' Throughout the study however, I attempted to become more and more precise. In the Baker case, for example, I compared three spontaneous listings, Marcus's, Jean's, and Amy's, to discover a ''core group of kinspersons.'' It was not until I had observed several interactions that I decided which people to carve out as the family: Amy Baker, her daughters, their children, and their children's children. The status of husbands, legal and/or ''common law,'' was much more ambiguous: they were of but not necessarily ''in'' the family.

When I showed the Bakers my rendition of their family in diagram form, the only person who had any qualms about it was Ann. She insisted that I put several of her cousins ''in the family.'' After months of observation, I myself had never even seen these cousins. Since I suffer from what may be called an ideological tendency to overextend, when I was in doubt, I left people out. Ann and I had several discussions about whether these cousins should be in or out, and she was even going to take me to Chicago Heights to meet them.

The night of Ann's anniversary party, I was sitting in

the kitchen eating when someone put Sister Sledge's "We are Family" on the stereo. I dropped my plate and ran to the dining room where the dancing was going on. There in the middle of the floor (actually taking up all the floor) were Ann and her seven sisters, as the vernacular would have it, "rockin' " and singing at the tops of their voices. "We are family. I've got all my sisters with me."

When the record stopped I approached Ann and said, "Hey, why don't you introduce me to those cousins you are always talking about. A look of utter dismay came over her face and she said, "I forgot to invite them." Ann and her husband had been planning this party for over a year. The invitations had been sent out a month in advance. If those cousins were indeed part of the family, they would not have been forgotten.

Summary

IN 1978 and 1979 the Baker family was extended. The set of intimate kin who participated in a system of mutual aid involving the exchange of goods and services extended across four generations and seven households. Residential proximity and involvement in daily exchanges were not prerequisites for membership in the Baker family. One Baker family household was located in another state and the other six were spread out over the entire Chicago black community. Though some members of the family interacted with others in face-to-face situations on a daily basis, most family members came together only once a week.

The composition of Baker family households was stable. Over the course of the initial study period the only changes in the composition of Baker family households involved one young man leaving to join the army and the birth of a new family member.

The Baker family was economically heterogeneous. Amy Baker raised her eight daughters on an income derived primarily from welfare payments. Amy and three of her daughters remained dependent on welfare. Four of Amy's daughter's, three of whom were married, were steadily employed for periods ranging from six to twenty-one years.

Exchanges between members of the Baker family were predominantly characterized by generalized reciprocity as indicated through the vagueness of the obligation to return goods and services of commensurate worth within a finite period of time. The generalized nature of the reciprocity involved in exchanges of goods and services between members of the Baker family was most explicit when the parties concerned differed in socioeconomic status. In the Baker family there was a great tolerance for one-way flows of goods and services from the haves to the have nots over long periods of time. The potential for conflict was mediated through the use of pooling as a redistributive mechanism. Goods and services were concentrated in the mother and redistributed through her.

The Bakers, 1982

SINCE my previous visit the Baker family had naturally increased by three members. Jean's daughters, Dette and Lynn, had each given birth and their Aunt Eve, one day after her thirtieth birthday had given birth to her first. My return to the Baker family was just in time to greet this newest member. When I arrived in Chicago, mother, son, and father were all recuperating at Amy Baker's house. In fact, Ann and her other sisters had already begun to wonder how much of a strain this arrangement was putting on Amy's resources. Ann said, "Now don't get me wrong, nobody minds feeding Eve or that baby. But that man! You should see how much he eats." The next week, "that man" gained both credibility and credit with the family by returning himself, "his woman," and their child to their own apartment and most importantly by making a token contribution to Amy out of his first paycheck from a new job.

The family had also expanded by three households. Not only was Eve living with her new child and his father, but Lynn (in Chicago) and Netta (in Milwaukee) had set up the same type of domestic arrangement. Dette, though pregnant again by the same young man, continued to live at home with her mother.

Since my last visit, Ben, like his cousin Marcus before him, had joined the army. This summer the family was quite excited by the prospect of having both of these young men home at the same time. The two cousins—one currently stationed in South Carolina and the other in Hawaii—had not seen each other for four years. For their reunion, Ann exclaimed, "We are going to pitch a 'wangdangdoodle.'" When it was discovered that simultaneous leaves could not be worked out and that once again the two young men would miss each other by less than a week, that was changed to "two wangdangdoodles"!

Though I too missed Ben, I did get a chance to see and talk with Marcus several times. When pressed by the family to say what I thought of him, I could only say that he had "grown to be a man." The Marcus that I met in

1978 had been deeply concerned about being unemployed and seemingly unemployable. He joined the service because welfare payments for his care had been stopped because of his age, and he could not bear to stay and eat the food that was meant for his younger brothers and sisters. In his own words he could not stand to take the food out of their mouths. This Marcus, "a sergeant," his mother exclaimed, had driven home in his own car. He brought money for his mother, Fourth of July firecrackers for his youngest brother, passed out dollar bills to small nieces, nephews, and cousins, and finally told his mother, "You keep this car, so that you can have transportation. I'll get myself another."

These developmental changes certainly cannot be interpreted as indicators of instability in the family nor do they seem to indicate that the composition of its component households is in a state of flux. The Baker family now has members in four states. The family remains economically heterogeneous.

While Amy, Christine, Jean, and Maxie continue to receive all or part of their incomes from government transfer payments, the other Baker sisters are employed. This heterogeneity, however, has not been static. If, for example, Marcus's economic position has improved, that of his Aunt Ann has deteriorated. Ann has not lost her job; in fact she has gotten several promotions and several raises and now earns "in the neighborhood of $30,000 a year." Ann's husband, Tom, however, was laid off from his job with a major airline shortly after the beginning of the PATCO strike in the fall of 1981. (He was called back to work in May of 1982, but worked only a month before he was again let go.) Ann estimates that their joint gross income for this year will suffer a $40,000 loss.

This loss of income does not appear to have affected the nature of Ann's relationship with the other members of her extended family, only its quantity. When things were going really good, that is, when both she and her husband were employed and she was moving up, she gave her mother at least $50 every payday ($100-$150 per month). Now, she says, "I can only give her about $20 each payday."

Ann explains that this has not greatly affected her mother's level of living. For though Eve, who still has her job with the City of Chicago, has moved out, Joclyn has started to work. Joclyn, Ann points out, does not make much money as a salesclerk in a Michigan Avenue shop— only slightly above minimum wage—and is often ill to the point of being hospitalized. But with what money Joclyn does make Ann says, "Her and Mama work miracles."

Ann certainly still performs other types of functions within the context of the family. The first weekend that I was in Chicago she kept every child in the family between the ages of two and eight (including Octavia who was down from Milwaukee to visit her great grandmother). "These," she says with obvious pride, "are my babies." It would be just as naive to think that these babies were just being kept as it would be to assume that Ann was getting nothing out of it.

The babies, as I discuss more fully in a later section, were being socialized to get along with each other, on neutral territory as it were, and with their Auntie Ann. Some of them were also learning how to function in a household with more and/or less of the accoutrements of a middle-class lifestyle than the household in which they normally reside. As for Ann, what she currently receives

FIGURE 5.3.
The Baker family, July 1982.

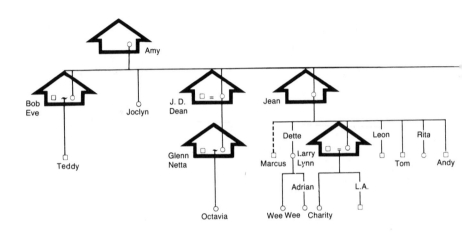

can be seen in her face every time she arrives at one of
their households and is greeted with a hug, a kiss, and
"Hey, there's Auntie Ann." She also confesses knowing
that by spending time with them now, while they are
small, though she has no children of her own, she does
not have to look forward to isolation in her old age. When
they are adults she will still be Auntie Ann, a member of
the family.

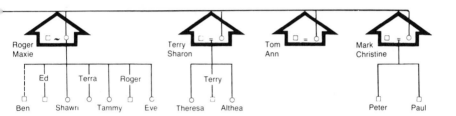

Key: ~ consensual union
     ○ female
     □ male
     = marriage
     -- not in any family household

Amy Baker's home is still the site for the family's weekend congregations, and she still functions as its redistributive center. She was performing this function when she allowed Eve to recuperate from childbirth in her house. She was able to do this partially because of what she and her children call her "Christmas." Amy points out that when her children were small, she was very, very poor. Even the older children can remember days when there was nothing for dinner but cornbread and heated canned peaches. Amy says that the worst day on which to have nothing good to eat is Christmas, so she began to stock nonperishable items to make sure that there would be something good on Christmas day. This stash of food became known as "Mama's Christmas." At one time, Amy points out, this Christmas occupied nothing more than a single shelf in a small white cabinet. It now occupies the largest portion of the basement of her house. It has almost the size and stock of a small neighborhood grocery store. For the Baker family "Christmas Day" has come to mean almost any day that you have to call upon the stock on mother's shelf or out of her freezer. Whenever they can, they help to replenish the stock.

Contributing goods and services to and receiving them from their mother is everyday stuff for the Baker sisters. What they wanted to talk about this summer was something a little more unusual. This summer the Baker family graduated another member from high school. In every Baker family household I entered there was a prominently displayed graduation and/or prom picture of Sharon's oldest daughter, Theresa. No matter what I had on the agenda, the first thing they wanted to discuss was her graduation and their hopes for her future.

Chapter 6
The Joneses

WHEN I first met Al Jones, who has been crippled by po-
lio since he was five, he was passed out on the ground outside my backdoor. Because there was a wheel chair behind him, I thought that maybe, just maybe, he was sick
rather than drunk and attempted to get close enough to
see if and how he was breathing. Before I reached him,
however, the old lady who was sitting on the back porch
next to mine pulled a gun out from under the towel she
was holding in her lap and warned me in no uncertain
terms that if I were to touch him she would blow my head
off.

I hurriedly tried to explain to her that my intentions
were to help rather than to hurt him and asked her if she
would like me to get him inside for her. The next time I
saw Al he was sober. While he was thanking me for helping his grandmother, I ascertained that he was thirty years

old, unmarried, and had been "raised on welfare." I
asked him to participate in my study and he agreed.

Interviewing Al, his grandmother, and his mother, I
uncovered a very small group of intimate kin who participate in a system of mutual aid involving the exchange of
goods and services. At the beginning of the research (September 1978), the Jones family included three households spanning three generations. Two of the households
were located in Chicago's Austin community area and
the third in the suburb of Schiller Park.

The first of the Austin households was headed by
Al's grandmother, Mrs. Carrie Jones. In this household
lived Al, his brother Thomas, his sister, Lea, and five unrelated males. The second Austin household contained
Al's sister Bobbie and her husband Terry. The household
in Schiller Park contained his mother, Mary, and her boyfriend Bill. By December, however, Bobbie's marriage
had dissolved, she had moved in with her mother in
Schiller Park, and given birth to a baby girl whom she
named Kelly. In December, Thomas was not living in any
family household.

In March, Mary's consensual arrangement with Bill
broke up and for a short period of time all members of the
Jones family were living in the household headed by Carrie Jones. By May, however, Mary had set up a new household. This new household was in the apartment building
located next door to the one in which Mrs. Jones lived.

Bobbie and Kelly moved into and lived primarily in
the new household which had been set up by Mary. Lea
and Thomas were dividing their time between the two
households, and Al continued to reside primarily with his
grandmother. In June, Mrs. Jones had moved into the
same building in which Mary's new apartment was lo-

FIGURE 6.1.

The Jones family, September 1978.

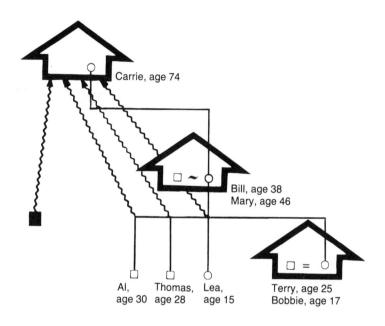

Carrie, age 74

Bill, age 38
Mary, age 46

Al,   Thomas,   Lea,
age 30   age 28   age 15

Terry, age 25
Bobbie, age 17

Key: ~ consensual union
  ○ female
  □ male
  = marriage
  -- not in any family household
  ⤳ residence not following line of descent
  ■ unrelated, transient male members of household

cated. This move, however, did not affect the residential distribution of the family members.

In the Jones family the individual on whom I concentrated was Al's mother, Mary. When the research began, Mary was living "fairly well" on the income she earned as a part-time cocktail waitress and on contributions made by the man with whom she was living. Once the research began, however, Mary's employment status changed several times. First she lost her job, and then she lost her man. She then got two jobs, one as a full-time cashier at Zayre's and the old part-time cocktail waitress position. She did all of this without relinquishing her welfare check. In addition to these sources of income, she also administered the Social Security check that Lea receives due to the death of her father. It became apparent after a while that Mary was not mobile in the sense that some members of the other families were. Every other adult in the family was being supported entirely by government transfer payments or had no visible means of support. Miss Carrie was getting her "old age pension," Al his "disability check," Bobbie a grant from Aid to Families with Dependent Children, and Thomas had no ascertainable source of income.

Until March of 1979 Mary lived in a western suburb of Chicago. While there was not actually much distance between Mary's apartment in Schiller Park and that of her mother in Austin they were not easily accessible to each other. Mary's apartment could not be reached by public transportation and no one in the family had a car. Whenever individuals wished to visit across households, they had to rely on friends or take taxis. Because Mrs. Jones at that time had no phone, Mary could not call her mother. Al and Lea, however, called Mary every day (using either the pay phone on the corner or a neighbor's phone). When Mary moved into the building next door to her mother, visiting between households was an almost daily occurrence. In addition, her mother had acquired a phone, and they talked to each other daily, sometimes several times a day. By the time Mrs. Jones moved into the same building with Mary, both of them had had their phone service disconnected for failure to pay the bill, and this form of interaction was no longer a part of their lives.

Mrs. Jones never visits Mary's household. When Mary lived in Schiller Park, Mrs. Jones explained that she did not go because she did not feel welcome. When they moved closer together she claimed that her arthritis and her asthma made it impossible for her to climb the three flights of stairs to Mary's apartment.

The exchanges of goods and services between Mary and the other members of her family tend to be characterized by balanced reciprocity. Mary allows her adult children to live with her, if, and only if, they are willing to pay their fair share. Mary will loan money to her mother and her children when they are short of cash. Such loans, however, are accompanied by a strict understanding about when and what amounts are to be paid back. The other members of the family complain that Mary seldom pays back what she borrows from them.

The day that Mrs. Jones moved I went to look at the new apartment. It was already dark and the door was opened by Mary holding a flashlight. When I asked to see Mrs. Jones, Mary took me to the living room window and showed me her mother sitting across the vacant lot in her old living room with her gun in her lap. If the purpose of the gun was to protect her property, then she was protect-

FIGURE 6.2.

The Jones family, December 1978.

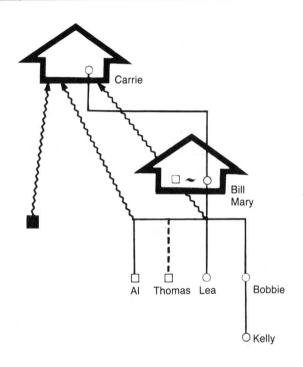

Carrie

Bill
Mary

Al Thomas Lea Bobbie

Kelly

Key: ～ consensual union
○ female
□ male
= marriage
-- not in any family household
➤ residence not following line of descent
■ unrelated, transient male members of household

ing it from the wrong people. Strangers had not broken into her new apartment, only her own daughter. Mary, with the aid of the flashlight, was going through her mother's belongings separating out what she wanted. As she found some object that she wanted, she put it in one of two groups. The first group was composed of large tables and lamps, things which she said she would later ask her mother to give her. The second group was composed of smaller things, like glasses, ashtrays, and candle holders, which she claimed her mother didn't need, would never miss, and which she planned to sneak out of the backdoor that very night.

It is Mary's children who serve to connect Mary and her mother. It is often difficult to tell in which of the households the children really live. They may sleep at Mary's one night and at Mrs. Jones' the next. They sometimes keep clothes in both places. Even Mary's visits to her mother involve the children—Lea should come upstairs and wash the dishes, Bobbie forgot the baby's bottle, some of Al's friends are having a fight in the living room.

Exchanges between these members of the family also most often involve balanced or negative reciprocity. Whenever money or other material goods initially change hands within the family, there is a clear statement (with witnesses brought into it) about how much or what is to be returned and when. "When" is most often on check day, which for federal monies is the first or third day of each month. On these days, several of the Joneses can be found in the front hallway waiting for the mailman and arguing about who owes what to whom. Each member of the family often accuses the others of trying to get something for nothing.

Though the Jones clearly cooperate with each other in securing shelter, the securing of food is an entirely individual matter. Each member of the family obtains and eats food separately. They do not even eat together on holidays. No member of the family buys more food than he or she can use in a short period of time. When members of the Jones family find themselves out of food and out of money, they can attempt to negotiate a loan from other members of the family, but they cannot expect to be fed. When they cannot find another member of the family willing to float a loan, members of the Jones family must find some other way of securing food or go hungry. Some members of the family buy on credit at a small neighborhood grocery while others beg for handouts from neighbors.

Two other noteworthy characteristics of the Jones family include the presence of nonrelatives in the household of Mrs. Carrie Jones and the absence of two of her children from the family. When I first interviewed Mrs. Jones, her three-room apartment was being shared with Al, Lea, Thomas, and five other males. Two of the household members who were not family members were teenage boys; the others were adults. One of the teenagers, Mike, was a runaway. His mother showed up several times when I was present to declare that his increasing delinquency was caused by the fact that he was allowed to hang out at Mrs. Jones's when he should have been in school. In the late fall, Mike was arrested for possession of stolen property and sent to a juvenile rehabilitation center. In the early spring he was allowed to go home for a leave and decided not to go back. Miss Carrie has allowed him to use her apartment as a place to hide from the police. The other teenage boy, Steve, is an orphan who refuses to stay in any of the foster homes to which the state assigns him. Mrs. Jones alternately claims and disclaims Steve as her grandson depending upon whether his excursions on the wrong side of the law have brought ready cash for him to share with her or brought the police, school authorities, or the landlord looking for him.

All of the adult males are what I have come to call "Miss Carrie's transients." These are men who bunk out in her living room—along with the rest of the family—on any of three couches, combinations of chairs, or the floor. The entire group sleeps fully clothed and some are without blankets even during the winter. The transients are there for a few days, maybe a week; then they are gone. Sometimes they come back again. Though the ostensible reason that they are allowed to stay is that they give Miss Carrie money for a place to sleep, one of her most frequent complaints is that when her transients have money they never come around.

In addition to her daughter, Mary, Carrie Jones gave birth to two sons. According to Miss Carrie, both of her sons upon graduating from high school were awarded basketball scholarships to college. Neither of them remained in college for a full year. The oldest son, Tom, dropped out of college during his freshman year to join the army, while Allen, the second son, dropped out to travel with the Harlem Globetrotters. Upon leaving college, both Allen and Tom severed their connections with their mother and sister.

According to Mrs. Jones, there were years during which her only clue to Tom's whereabouts were the postmarks on the Christmas and Mother's Day cards he sent to her, while the best indicators of Allen's whereabouts were press releases from the Globetrotter public relations office. Carrie Jones still remembers how the other employees at a nursing home where she once worked were reluctant to believe that the handsome Allen, whom they paid to go see, was really her son. (I myself have doubts about this story, but will report what was told to me.)

When Mrs. Jones became ill and unable to work, she looked to her fellow employees and friends for help. They told her to get it from those sons of hers that she was always talking about. Her entreaties to Tom for aid were responded to by letters which explained that he simply had no money to send her. Her pleas to Allen came back unopened.

After Tom married and began to have children, Mrs. Jones felt she could expect no more from him. From a still single Allen she expected much more. In desperation, she says, she wrote to Abe Saperstein, owner-manager of the Globetrotters, explaining her situation. Until she was able to go back to work, her rent was paid every month. According to her, Mr. Saperstein took the $60 out of her son's paycheck each month and sent it directly to her landlord.

At the time of his death ten years ago, Allen still had not reestablished close contact with his mother or sister. His now adult children live in the nearby suburb of Maywood and never call or come visit their grandmother. (Occasionally Bobbie or Lea go to visit these cousins. I have even seen the cousins drive up in front of Miss Carrie's building, blow the horn for their cousin to come out, and never come in to say hello to their grandmother.)

Upon retiring from the army, Tom settled with his wife and children in the same small Arkansas town in which he had been born and from which his mother had migrated with her three small children. He established contact with his mother and even invited her to come and live with him. Mrs. Jones went to Arkansas, but the trip turned out to be a visit rather than a move. According to Miss Carrie, she could not stay with her son and his family because they think they are better than she is. Though Tom occasionally writes his mother, he will not send her any money. He tells her that if she really needed help, she would come and live with him.

No member of the Jones family attends church regularly. According to Mrs. Jones, she was an active member of a Missionary Baptist church until she was publicly censured for having an affair with a married man. In Carrie's view, the censure was nothing more than an exercise in hypocrisy. Carrie claims that not only did the church realize that she needed that man to help take care of her children, but in singling her out for censure they passed over other members who had higher profiles as both church members and sinners.

Mary admits that her regular attendance at church ended with her mother's and that she never took her children or insisted that they go. Bobbie and Lea both admit that their occasional trips to church are motivated more by the desire to engage in a social event and to show off new clothes than for the edification of their souls.

Summary

THE Jones family was extended. The set of intimate kin who participated in a system of mutual aid involving the exchange of goods and services spanned four generations and usually included more than one household.

Residential proximity and involvement in daily exchanges were not requisite for membership in the Jones family. When family members lived near each other, they tended to interact face to face daily. When distance intervened, however, the telephone became the primary mode through which interaction occurred.

Household composition in the Jones family was extremely unstable. Not only did individual family members shuttle back and forth between households, but the number of households changed several times. At the beginning of the study there were three Jones family households. When one household collapsed due to the breakup of a marriage, family members were absorbed into one of the other two existing households. When one of these households could no longer be maintained due to the breakup of a consensual union, all members of the family shared a single household. By the end of the initial study period a second household had been established. At least one Jones family household often contained unrelated individuals who moved in and out randomly.

The Jones family was not economically heterogeneous. The sons of Carrie Jones, the two potential family members who had experienced some mobility, had isolated themselves from the other members of the family to such an extent that they could not be considered members of the family. The only member of the Jones family who was employed during the study was not stably employed. Mary Jones, though she was willing to work at two jobs for short periods of time, had never been able to work steadily enough to remove herself from the welfare rolls.

Because Mary never gave family members anything without getting back an equivalent amount, her failure to be mobile cannot be attributed to involvement with her children and mother. In fact, exchanges between all

FIGURE 6.3.
The Jones family, June 1979.

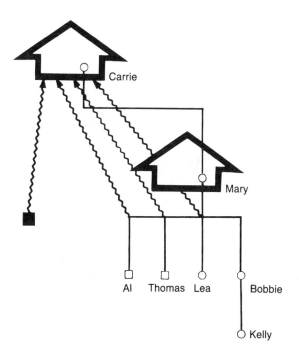

Key: ~ consensual union
  ○ female
  □ male
  = marriage
  -- not in any family household
  ⤳ residence not following line of descent
  ■ unrelated, transient male members of household

members of the Jones family were predominantly characterized by balanced reciprocity, wherein exchanges of
goods and services between kin stipulated returns of commensurate worth or utility within a finite period of time.
Members of the Jones family even attempted to get something for nothing from each other with impunity. Attempts at such negative reciprocity were not heavily sanc-
tioned by other members of the family.

Pooling as a mechanism of redistribution was almost
totally absent from the relationships among members of
the Jones family. Though they cooperated with each
other in the securing shelter, they shared little else.

The Joneses, 1982

THOUGH they were the family I most wanted to see in
1982, I simply could not locate the Jones family. I went to
their old apartment building, their old school, their old
church, their old places of employment, and even to the
places where they just used to hang out. Anyone who had
information about the whereabouts of the Joneses was
not giving it out to me.

Chapter 7
Commonalities and Differences

WHEN boundaries are defined in terms of kinship and mutual assistance, each of the four families discussed here exhibits an external structure most adequately described as extended. In each case the family identified and described spanned three to four generations and was spread out over several households. Perhaps the best way to examine their other commonalities and differences is through some of the points of disagreement in the literature.

The boundaries which various authors have seen as delimiting the structure of black extended families are clearly reflected in their divergent definitions. After spending three years in the field to discover how the black urban poor adapt to poverty, Carol Stack "ultimately . . . defined family as the smallest, organized, durable network of kin and nonkin who interact daily, providing the domestic needs of children and assuring their survival''

(1974:31). Elmer and Joanne Martin, on the other hand say, "When we speak of a black extended family, we mean a multigenerational, interdependent kinship system which is welded together by a sense of obligation to relatives; is organized around a 'family base' household; is generally guided by a 'dominant family figure'; extends across geographical boundaries to connect family units to an extended family network; and has a built in mutual aid system for the welfare of its members and the maintenance of the family as a whole" (1978:1). Although some members of the families compared here lived very close to each other, residential proximity and daily interaction were not requisite for family membership. Two of the four families, at both points in time, had family members who lived in different states. Neither did close residential proximity of kin insure membership in the family. In no case did the family contain every available kin-related person. Instead, there was a high degree of consistency in how genealogical connection was utilized to abstract the "family" from the universe of kin. With several minor variations (e.g., the number of generations and the presence of spouses in any generation) these families consisted of a woman, her children, and her grandchildren. As suggested by Sudarkasa (1981) and Aschenbrenner (1975) the core of these families was consanguineous. As Martin and Martin (1978) suggest, however, each of these families did keep up some connection with a larger kinship network.

It was only in the case of the Jones family that any of the women's children were missing from the family or any fictive kin putatively present within it.

Another question which has arisen about black extended families concerns the stability of their component households. While Valentine (1978) has been content to say that members of these families, especially children, frequently move from one household to another, Stack (1974) has suggested that "residential flux" is so great in lower-class black communities that the household has become a meaningless unit of analysis. During the initial research year each family in this study experienced some changes in the composition of component households. In only one case, again that of the Jones family, were these changes frequent or far-reaching enough to be termed residential flux.

Compositional changes in the Baker family involved nothing more than a young man joining the army and the birth of a new family member. In the Edmonds family adolescents transferred from one family household to a family household located in a different state. In the Niles' case adolescents moved from a family household (the mother's) to a household which was part of another extended family (the father's) in which they held simultaneous membership.

In the Jones family not only did individuals shuttle back and forth between households but the number of households changed several times. At the beginning of the study period there were three Jones family households. When one household broke up due to the collapse of a marriage, family members were absorbed into one of the existing family households. When this household collapsed due to the breakup of a consensual union, all family members resided for a short while in a single household. By the end of the study period a second household had again been established.

The relative stability of the Niles, Edmonds, and Baker families is clearly demonstrated by the fact that the only changes in their composition and the composition of their component households between June of 1979 and July of 1982 were developmental changes. In the Niles family, both Tina and her daughter had married and were living apart from one another, while Tina's two sisters had each given birth to another child. In the Edmonds family, Karen and Ed had produced another child, Salena had reconciled with her husband, and Steve had gotten a more expensive apartment in a better part of town (and a roommate to share expenses). The Baker family over the course of this time had increased naturally by three members, its young women had set up three additional households, and another of its young men had joined the army. In these three families neither the address nor telephone number of what Martin and Martin (1978) might call the "family base household" had changed since my previous visit. The Jones family on the other hand could not be located.

Disagreements have also arisen over whether black extended families are economically heterogeneous. Stack (1974) noted that those kin who were doing fairly well had isolated themselves from the third generation welfare recipients she studied. The Martins (1978) on the other hand found that in each of the extended families they studied there were some individuals who had achieved middle-class status. The responses of these individuals and their families to their mobility took three distinct patterns. First, there were individuals whose middle-class status was so precarious that they were unable to contribute financially to their families' mutual aid systems. As long as they kept in regular contact, however, their families seemed satisfied that they were at least not an economic drain on the system and highly satisfied that, while being able to make it on their own, the mobiles had not lost their sense of family.

Secondly, there were a few individuals who upon achieving middle-class status had cut themselves off from their extended families. They refused to participate in the system of mutual aid even though they were financially able. Family opinion was likely to be divided on how these individuals should be treated. While some relatives felt that regardless of an individual's behavior he or she was still part of the family, others felt that such individuals had removed themselves from the family and looked down on their less well-off kin.

The third and most common response, however, was to continue to participate in the mutual aid system of the extended family. Mobiles made small but regular cash contributions to the family, were the first to offer help to relatives in emergency situations, and provided many forms of nonfinancial assistance to the other members of their extended families. Their families in turn identified with their success and accorded them status without seeing them as belonging to a different social class.

Each of the responses identified by the Martins (1978) was found in the families described here. Only the Jones family, however, was isolated from potential members who had experienced some mobility. As a result only the Jones family was economically homogeneous—homogeneously poor. Throughout the initial study period only one member of the Jones family, Mary, was employed at all, and her employment was both part-time and temporary. The poverty of the Jones family was reflected in the almost total reliance of its members on government transfer payments as a means of subsistence. The other three families were economically heteroge-

FIGURE 7.1.

The flow of goods and services through the mutual aid systems of economically undifferentiated underclass families.

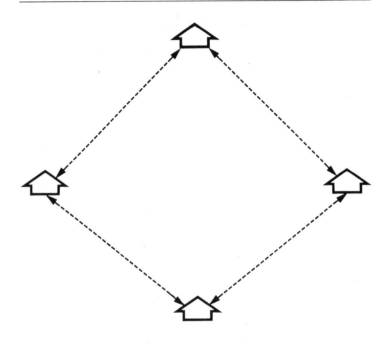

Key: 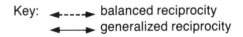 balanced reciprocity

generalized reciprocity

FIGURE 7.2.

The flow of goods and services through the mutual aid systems of economically differentiated families.

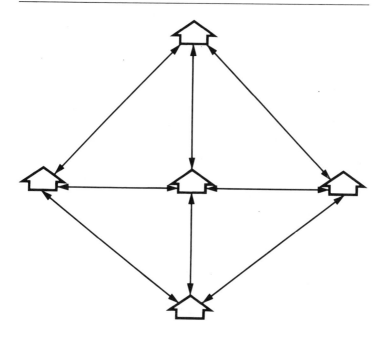

Key: 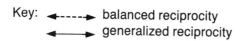 balanced reciprocity
generalized reciprocity

neous. At the very least this meant that while some members of the family were dependent on government subsidies other members of the families were at least steadily employed. In fact, the economic heterogeneity of these families was so extreme that if income were used as the only measure of social class these families would have to be seen as being composed of individuals who differ in social class. In 1982, the Niles, Edmonds, and Baker families were still economically heterogeneous.

Moreover, whether a family was economically heterogeneous or homogeneously poor appeared to influence the style of interpersonal relationships between family members and to produce variations in their systems of mutual aid. Stack (1974:43) concluded that "gift exchange is the style of interpersonal relationship by which local coalitions of cooperating kinsmen distinguish themselves from other blacks—those low income and working class blacks who have access to steady employment." The initial observations of the four families described here suggested rather that "gift exchange" is the style of interpersonal relationship by which coalitions of homogeneously poor kinsmen distinguish themselves from coalitions of kinsmen who are economically heterogeneous.

Variations in Interdependencies

THROUGHOUT the entire observation period I concentrated on trying to understand who did what for whom, how often they did it, what they expected, and what they received in return. The interdependencies between family members were initially conceived of as a series of exchanges involving the vice-versa movements of goods and services between two parties, and I began by concentrating on current exchanges which I either witnessed or was informed of.[1] For purposes of analysis these exchanges were then categorized in terms of where they tended to fall on Sahlins "Spectrum of Reciprocities"[2] (1965:147). Briefly, Sahlin has proposed, and not without controversy, a spectrum of reciprocities for general use which is defined by its extremes and its midpoint:

1. At one extreme lies "generalized reciprocity" which "refers to transactions that are putatively altruistic, transactions on the line of assistance given and, if possible and necessary returned."
2. At the midpoint lies "balanced reciprocity" which "refers to direct exchange. In precise balance, the reciprocation is the customary equivalent of the thing given and without delay."
3. At the other extreme is "negative reciprocity" or "attempts to get something for nothing with impunity."

In every case but the Jones family, exchanges between members tended to fall at that extreme of the spectrum defined by generalized reciprocity. Exchanges were constantly being made without clear-cut obligations to return goods and services of commensurate worth within a finite period of time. One-way flows of goods and services were tolerated for long periods of time, and the material aspect of the transfer was definitely subordinate to the social.

On the other hand, exchanges between members of the Jones family tended to fall near the midpoint of the spectrum defined as balanced reciprocity. Exchanges between members of this family always carried clear stipulations that returns of commensurate worth were expected within a finite period of time. One-way flows of goods and services were simply not tolerated. In addition, members of the Jones family often tried and were sometimes successful at getting something from each other for nothing. Only in the case of the Jones family was I able to see clear instances where exchanges were characterized by negative reciprocity. Moreover, it was only in the case of the Jones family that the system of mutual aid could be understood by looking only at the vice-versa movements of goods and services between individual family members. In each of the other cases there were also interdependencies among family members which created a mutual aid system characterized by a network of both direct and indirect exchanges.

The primary process through which the mutual aid systems of these families provided for the indirect flow of goods and services from one family member to another was pooling. To a limited extent, each of these families except the Joneses practiced pooling. This is not to say that the members of these families put their incomes into one pot from which the needs of all family members were met. However, they did tend to concentrate goods and services on a central person in such a way that they could be redistributed according to need.

In the Baker, Niles, and Edmonds families, the mother had in a sense become the central storehouse. All family members made contributions to her. This was done with the knowledge that her storehouse could be drawn upon whenever one was in need. It seems fair to say that the members of these families felt obligated to make contributions to their mother when they were able to do so. They also felt free to call upon her for aid and to remain in her debt for long periods of time. Members of

TABLE 7.1.
The range of incomes per family, 1978–1979.

Family	Lowest Monthly Income	Highest Monthly Income	Income Difference
Edmonds	Salena $300	Gladys $2,000	$1,700
Niles	Brenda $300	Lettie $4,166	$3,866
Baker	Jean $500	Tom $2,916	$2,416
Jones	Al $200	Mary $500	$200

these families argued, in fact, that no matter how much one gave one's mother, one remained eternally in her debt. The implied wisdom seemed to be that since you could never pay your mother back, it was perfectly acceptable to continue to borrow from her as well as to give to her.

The mothers in these families received goods from all directions and redistributed them in all directions, making sure that at any point in time the main direction of the flow was from the haves to the have nots. Even when they themselves were poor these mothers often took contributions from one or more family members and immediately transferred all or part of it to family members currently in need. In the Jones family there was no central storehouse.

These differences can be clearly seen in each family's food related behavior. The members of three of these families organized a great deal of their time around the sharing of food. They carried gifts of food from one household to another and they cooked and ate together both when necessity dictated and ritualistically. In each of these cases the credo seemed to be that espoused by Mrs. Edmonds, ''No member of my family will ever go hungry as long as there is anything that I can do about it.'' For the Joneses, the securing of food was an entirely individual matter. Each member of the family obtained and ate their own food separately. They did not even eat together on holidays. No member of the family bought more food than they could use themselves in a short period of time. When a member of the Jones family found themselves out of food and out of money, they could attempt to float a loan from some other member of the family, but they could not expect to be fed. When they could not find another member of the family willing to float them a loan, members of the Jones family either went hungry or found some other way of securing food for themselves. They bought on credit at a small neighborhood grocery and begged for handouts from neighbors.

The observations of these four families suggest that their interdependencies fall into two modes. In one mode (that exemplified by the Bakers, the Niles, and the Edmonds) exchanges between family members were characterized by generalized reciprocity, and family members engaged in a limited form of pooling. In the other mode, that exemplified by the Jones, exchanges between family members were characterized by balanced reciprocity, and pooling behavior was absent.

In order to explore what factors were associated with the mode of interdependencies in these four families, they were compared along several dimensions which various authors have suggested meaningfully allow black families to be compared to each other. These include: (1) the urban/rural, Northern/Southern dichotomies (Billingsley, 1968); (2) the orientation of the family toward religion and law (Drake and Cayton, 1945); (3) the cultural adaptation of the family (Bernard, 1966); (4) the developmental phase of the family (Aschenbrenner, 1973) and (5) social class.

The rural Southern origins of the Jones family was not unique among the families in the study. The Joneses were no more nor less religious than the other families. Members of the Jones family did not favor engaging in "shady" activities to a greater extent than the members of the other families.[3] The four-generation developmental phase of the family was shared with two of the other families in the study. Neither did the Jones appear to exist in a different cultural reality from the rest of the families; though they did not practice generalized reciprocity or pooling, they did espouse them "as the way things ought to be" and recognized that they had somehow lost that "diffuse enduring solidarity" which is supposed to exist among the members of a family.

The lack of generalized reciprocity within the Jones family in fact seems explainable in fairly simple terms. That is, there can be no one-way flows of goods and services from the haves to the have nots when there are no haves. The Jones, as a family, were poorer than the other families observed and found themselves in a position

TABLE 7.2.
Distribution of Niles, Edmonds, Baker, and Jones family households located in Chicago by community area, June 1979.

Family	Household	Community Area
Niles	1. Lettie Niles	41. Hyde Park
	2. Tina Niles	43. South Shore
	3. Edward Niles	69. Greater Grand Crossing
	4. Louise Niles	42. Woodlawn
	5. Brenda Niles	71. Auburn Gresham
Edmonds	1. Gladys Edmonds	Not in city
	2. Mamie Edmonds	29. North Lawndale
	3. Karen Edmonds	29. North Lawndale
	4. Steve Edmonds	29. North Lawndale
	5. Ed Edmonds	29. North Lawndale
Baker	1. Amy Baker	67. West Englewood
	2. Dean Baker	Not in city
	3. Jean Baker	54. Riverdale
	4. Maxie Baker	75. Morgan Park
	5. Sharon Baker	56. Garfield Ridge
	6. Ann Baker	25. Austin
	7. Christine Baker	43. South Shore
Jones	1. Alberta Jones	25. Austin
	2. Bobbie Jones	25. Austin

where not to directly repay meant that someone else would go hungry. I still have no clear understanding of why the Joneses did not pool their resources to a greater extent. It did occur to me, however, that perhaps it is true that in order for pooling to appear as a redistributive mechanism a surplus must exist.

The descriptions of the variations in the interdependencies between members of lower-class urban black extended families presented here are certainly not meant to be exhaustive. These descriptions do serve to point out that those who would seek to enhance the functioning of these support systems, as well as those who would uncover factors which have a negative impact on them, must be attuned to the variations within them.

The 1978–1979 observations had led me to believe that it was those members of these families who were stably employed who were providing the "safety net" for those members of their families who remained dependent on government transfer payments. Initially, I saw no further safety net for the Jones family. I felt that if the Jones family "got any poorer," it would cease to exist as a functioning social system. Eventually, I came to feel that, even if the Jones family, as I had empirically identified it, was to have "disintegrated" over the past four years, its individual members may very well have survived. This was suggested by the fact that the members of each of the other families did keep in touch with larger kin groupings and often drew their own intimate kin from distinct pools of relatives. It may be that when an empirically existing family reaches a point of "discontinuity," individual members may be absorbed into families which have not reached the limits of their resources. Nobles (1978) has suggested that this type of behavior is characteristic of black families.

Since the complete lack of 1982 data on the Jones family precludes further comment on these speculations, I propose that future research could and should be designed which does in fact address them. As is discussed in the next chapter, the existence of these variations has some bearing on controversies surrounding the origins and consequences of black family patterns.

Chapter 8
Origins and Consequences

THOUGH it is rapidly becoming general knowledge that extensive kinship is characteristic of black social structure, until the 1950s American sociology was little concerned with the relations among kin. "In the 1930s and 1940s leading scholars were writing confidently that the American family was nuclear and isolated" (Winch, 1977:12). There is little wonder then that E. Franklin Frazier's classical studies of black family life which were also written during this time period (1931; 1939) concentrated on attempting to explain the origins and consequences of black domestic families, particularly the mother/child domestic unit, or that they mention extended kinship only in passing.[1]

Concern with black extended kinship had its origin in responses to Moynihan's (1965) thesis which emphasized the causal effect of family form on the economic progress of blacks as a group.[2] Moynihan's conclusions were quite clear. As a consequence of or adaptation to poverty and discrimination blacks had developed a family structure different from the conjugal-nuclear form which was considered to be the norm in American society. Black family structure, however important it may have been for survival in earlier time periods, was now to be seen as a barrier which prevented blacks from escaping poverty. Moynihan wrote: "At the heart of the deterioration of the fabric of Negro society is the deterioration of the Negro family" (1965:5). "In essence the Negro community has been forced into a matriarchal structure which, because it is so out of line with the rest of American society, seriously retards the progress of the group as a whole." (1965:29).

In response to this thesis black social scientists presented what they considered to be objective, nondeficit views of the black family. Several of these authors (Hill, 1971; Ladner, 1972; Billingsley, 1968) shared the theme that black domestic families were not isolated from kin and that the extended kin provided sources of support which allowed black individuals not only to cope and survive but sometimes to prosper in American society.

Some writers, however, after they "discovered" black involvement with the extended kin, have only been able to explain its existence as an adaptation to conditions of urban poverty. Moreover, in a fashion very similar to Moynihan's concern with the "matriarchy," some writers see black involvement with the extended kin as an adaptation which must be forsaken if mobility is to be achieved. This view is clearly expressed in the work of Carol Stack (1974).

After spending three years in the field to discover how the black poor adapt to poverty, Stack reported finding that domestic functions are carried out by clusters of kin who may or may not live together. The basis of these networks included the exchanges of goods and services between kin. Stack observed that (much like the Jones family) the third-generation welfare recipients in her study found their bare subsistence needs so large in comparison to their incomes that it was impossible for them to meet their survival needs without assistance from relatives. According to Stack, once the requirements for survival were met through the cooperation of the kin network, those helped were strongly obligated to repay, unable to conceal any resources they might obtain, and thereby prevented from securing the financial basis for upward mobility. Stack noted that those who were doing fairly well had isolated themselves from their kin living in poorer circumstances. She concluded that the cooperation between members of these networks both had its genesis in and served to perpetuate conditions of urban poverty.

The economic heterogeneity of three of the families discussed here certainly calls into question the idea that involvement with the extended kin and social mobility are antithetical.[3] The findings here are more consistent with those of Harriette McAdoo (1975, 1977, 1978, 1979, 1980, 1981). McAdoo's interviews with eighty-eight urban and ninety suburban middle-class domestic families revealed that they too engage in interaction and mutual helping activities with their kin. While some of the parents in these families had been middle class for a generation or more, the majority of them had in three successive generations moved from poverty to the working class and then to middle-class status. All the parents interviewed had received aid from their kin which helped

them to achieve their middle-class status. They continued to "keep in close touch with their parents, brothers
and sisters, and other kin, giving and receiving substantial kinds of help" (1979:67).

Since kin helping behavior occurs among members
of the black middle class as well as among those living at
the lowest socioeconomic levels, McAdoo dismisses the
notion that cooperation with kin can be treated as merely
a strategy developed to cope with poverty. While admit-
ting that for mobiles, continued participation in the mutual aid system of their extended families may operate as
a kind of insurance, she also argues that the persistence of
patterns of mutual aid after some degree of prosperity has
been reached indicates that mutual aid between kin is a
viable attribute of Afro-American culture.

The persistence of kin involvement after some degree of prosperity has been reached is not the only factor
which suggests that black involvement with the extended
kin is a cultural attribute rather than an adaptation to
conditions of urban poverty. Another element is the fact
that the extended family pattern appears to predate the
large scale urbanization of blacks.

The Black Family: An Historical Perspective

ALTHOUGH the historical relationship between the
present-day blacks of the United States and Africa is obvious, there has been an enduring controversy surrounding
the survival and influence of African cultural heritage in
the New World. The issue of whether African culture has
influenced the family life of black Americans is not iden-
tical to, but finds its place within, this larger debate.

Noting that "considerable attention has been given to this controversy . . . probably less for the merit of the arguments than for the political implications of the issues" (Whitten and Szwed, 1970:28), no attempt is made here to adopt and defend a single position. This discussion attempts rather to convey the changing nature and context of the arguments and their implications for the origins of black involvement with the extended kin.

Traditional scholarly opinion presented a fairly homogeneous conception concerning African survivals in the United States. Specialists tended to accept the view that as a result of the pressures exerted by the experience of slavery, all aboriginal modes of thought and behavior disappeared in the United States. E. Franklin Frazier, perhaps the most renowned of black family specialists, stressed this position. "Probably never before in history has a people been so nearly completely stripped of its social heritage as the Negroes who were brought to America. Other conquered races have continued to worship their household gods within the intimate circle of their kinsmen. But American slavery destroyed household gods and dissolved the bonds of sympathy and affection between men of the same blood and household" (1966:15).

According to Frazier, slaves from different tribes and language groups were mixed in the caravans in Africa and during the Middle Passage. Once they reached America, Frazier felt that the slaves were broken up into even smaller groups before being sent to the plantations. "Through force of circumstances, they had to acquire a new language, adopt new habits of labor, and take over, however imperfectly, the folkways of the American environment" (1966:15).

Frazier felt that where the slaves, as in the case of house servants, were able to closely observe the familial behaviors of their masters, they also adopted their own masters' familial values. He felt that when the ability to observe was accompanied by freedom, blacks also exhibited these values in their behavior. For the mass of slaves, however, he felt that social isolation prevented them from being able to adopt their masters' values while the constraints of the slave system prevented them from copying their behavior.

Frazier also felt that other factors worked to keep the mass of slaves from developing a family system which could be viewed as stable. He argued that initially the loss of African cultures as guidelines and the unbalanced sex ratio (many more men than women) encouraged sexual contacts based only on individual desires. Even after the system of slavery had stabilized and guidelines for sexual behavior were handed down by masters, Frazier felt that these guidelines were not constructed to insure the development of stable nuclear families. He felt that many slaveholders sexually exploited black women regardless of their marital status or familial ties. Frazier also felt that the structure of slave families was affected by the fact that male slaves, because they were unable to own property or secure incomes, were unable to guarantee support for their wives and children and were unable to hold authority over them.

Under these conditions, Frazier believed, a maternal family system developed: "Only the bond between the mother and her child continually resisted the disruptive effect of economic interests that were often inimical to family life among the slaves. Consequently, under all conditions of slavery, the Negro mother remained the most dependable and important figure in the family'' (1966:32). In sum, Frazier concluded that slavery had so destroyed African social patterns that the familial and kin arrangements of Negro Americans could be viewed only as attempts to imitate white family patterns. The success of the imitation, in Frazier's view, depended on the degree to which the slave was able to observe the behavior of the master and the extent to which he was able to escape the requirements of the slave system.

Melville J. Herskovits, an anthropologist, took an exception to this view of survivals and their influence on black family life. In his *The Myth of the Negro Past,* Herskovits (1958) focused on similarities among the cultures of Negro peoples in various social and economic situations. When he discovered similarities, he termed them ''Africanisms.'' Herskovits explained the continuity of African cultural forms in terms of the process of retention; somehow, components of African life had been retained through several centuries of slavery and oppression. Where he did not find clear-cut retentions but still felt that the differences between black and white cultural patterns required historical explanation, he referred to a process of ''reinterpretation.'' His third term, '' syncretism,'' refers to the synthesis of African and European cultures into the creation of a new form. Whereas Frazier was committed to the idea that there were no African cultural elements in black family patterns, Herskovits saw the female-centered household and serial marriages as ''reinterpretations'' of African polygyny in the New World. Frazier, on the other hand, termed those specific African survivals revealed by Herskovits and others as remarkable exceptions whose existence served only to highlight the almost total cultural destruction wrought by slavery (Whitten and Szwed, 1970).

Though Herskovits was the most widely known of Frazier's critics on the subject of African cultural survivals, he was by no means the first to recognize the need to study the family life of American blacks against an African background. As early as 1908, W. E. B. Du Bois had written in his work on the black family: "In each case an attempt has been made to connect present conditions with the African past. This is not because Negro-Americans are Africans, or can trace an unbroken social history from Africa, but because there is a distinct nexus between Africa and America which, though broken and perverted, is nevertheless not to be neglected by the careful student" (1908:9). In a similar vein, Carter G. Woodson argued that to ignore the African past and/or to assume that it was not worth studying because someone had said so, was to contribute to the continuing "miseducation of the Negro."

Since the time of the debate between Frazier and Herskovits, compromise positions have developed. One position suggests that Herskovits, rather than being entirely wrong, merely overstated his case in the area of social organization. Proponents of this view (Kiel, 1966; Blassingame, 1972; Rawick, 1972) suggest that we accept Frazier's position on the family as a refutation of only that portion of Herskovits' work which suggests any simple retention or direct continuity between African and Afro-American family forms. "On the other hand, basic African predispositions governing religion and esthetics not only survived slavery, but were reshaped, nurtured, and magnified in response to slavery and post slavery conditions. The facts that support this statement are available to anyone who will read *The Myth of the Negro Past''* (Kiel, 1966:5).

Like Frazier, others who discount the possibility of African cultural survivals have done so at least partially in terms of the cultural diversity of the African peoples who were enslaved. At one time this meant accepting the notion that slave trails ran more than a thousand miles inland and that slaves were derived from all of sub-Saharan Africa. Since it is now generally accepted that though few African peoples completely escaped the slave trade, the majority of those enslaved came from West Africa (Herskovits, 1958; Davidson, 1961), current disclaimers tend to expound upon the cultural diversity to be found in this area alone. Billingsley, for example, points out that there were at least three basic patterns of descent reckoning in West Africa alone: "The Ibo of Eastern Nigeria, the Yoruba of Western Nigeria, and their neighbors, the Dahomeans, were patrilineal. The Ashanti of Ghana were matrilineal. The Yanko people (of Nigeria) practiced double descent" (1968:40).

Those who accept the possibility of survivals replace the emphasis on diversity with an emphasis on the cultural similarity of the enslaved peoples. Herskovits claimed "a sufficient degree of similarities in the cultures of the entire area so that a slave from any part of it would find little difficulty in adapting himself to whatever specific forms of African behavior he might encounter in the New World" (1958:78). Sudarkasa (1981) argues that lineages, large coresidential domestic groups, and polygynous marriages were almost universal features of kinship organization in that part of western Africa from which the enslaved originated. Nobles (1974) proposes that this similarity took the form of an African world view, an "ethos." "This author contends that African peoples share in these basic beliefs: the survival of the tribe and the tribe being in an indispensable unity with nature. It is further suggested that this ethos is coupled with several philosophical principles, i.e. unity, cooperative effort, mutual responsibility, etc. which influence most, if not every aspect of Black social reality" (1974:55).

As we have seen, however, the acceptance or rejection of survivals as influencing black family life lies not only in accepting or rejecting the notion of some binding commonality in West African life, but also in how we view the nature of American slavery and the adaptation of the enslaved to it.

While no attempt is made here to suggest that the classical interpretations of American slavery were uniform, it does appear that many scholars tended to agree with Frazier about slavery's effects on Negro family life. This perspective holds that Africans, violently wrenched from their own societies, were thrust into a new situation which not only failed to provide support for traditional African forms, but actually discouraged the establishment of new ones (Bryce-La Porte, 1969; Green, 1975; Clarke, 1975).

Since slaves were property, they were denied the legal right to marry. "Their condition was compatible only with a form of concubinage 'voluntary' on the part of slaves and permissive on that of masters" (Stampp, 1956:198). This condition has led many scholars to conclude that conjugal ties were weak and of little consequence to slaves or their masters (Bernard, 1966). It has been asserted that in many cases masters broke up families as financial need dictated, utilized slaves in breeding programs, and sexually exploited female slaves (Elkins, 1959; Wade, 1964). Elkins (1959) in fact argues that the shock of enslavement and the requirements for existence within the closed slave system left the individual slaves perpetually marooned in an unending childhood.

The revisionist history of the 1970s, also partially sparked by Moynihan's (1965) report, offers new views of the effect of plantation slavery on the family lives of black people. Although these revised views of American slavery can be roughly and simplistically divided into those which allow for the existence of a viable slave family by emphasizing a more benign view of slavery and those which emphasize the adaptive capacity of the enslaved, the consistencies between them suggest that for all their debate neither Frazier nor Herskovits captured the nature of the slave family.

One of the most controversial reinterpretations was written by Fogel and Engerman (1974). Attempting to dispute not what they considered to be myths about the black family, but rather what they considered to be myths about the political economy of slavery itself, Fogel and Engerman (1974:5) say "The belief that slave breeding, sexual exploitation, and promiscuity destroyed the black family is a myth." The slave system, they say (in most direct contrast to Genovese (1975), was neither economically moribund on the eve of the Civil War, nor irrationally kept in existence by plantation owners who failed to perceive or were indifferent to their own best interests. Since the family on most large plantations was: (1) the administrative unit for the distribution of food, clothing, and shelter; (2) an instrument for maintaining labor discipline; and (3) the main instrument for promoting the increase of the slave population, it was in the economic interests of planters to encourage the stability of slave families and most of them did so.

While Fogel and Engerman agree that slave marriages were explicitly forbidden by the legal codes of the states, they emphasize that these marriages were recognized and promoted under plantation codes. According to these authors the slave family was not only stable, but also nuclear and patriarchal. ''Planters recognized husbands as the head of the family. Slave families were listed in their books with husband at the top of the lists. Houses were assigned by the names of the husbands and the semiannual issue of clothing to families were made in the name of the husband. Garden patches were assigned to the husbands and the money earned from the sale of crops from these patches was held in his name'' (1974:142). For Fogel and Engerman, if the slaves abandoned African family forms it was not because of the harshness of the middle passage or because masters broke up families, but because these forms did not meet the needs of blacks who lived and worked under far different conditions than their ancestors had.

Eugene Genovese's (1974;1978) view of the world in which the slaves lived is not quite as benign as that of Fogel and Engerman. Nevertheless, for Genovese the world the slaves made cannot be separated from the world made by their masters. He argues that though slavery did take a terrible toll ''the slaves created impressive norms of family, including as much of a nuclear family norm as conditions permitted'' (1978:36). Genovese claims that because they increasingly lived on their plantations American slaveholders found it necessary to construct a world in which both black and white could live as well as work. The masters, he says, justified their use of slaves' unpaid labor as a fair return for their protection of the slave. The slaves on the other hand were able to interpret this "paternalism" in such a way as to preserve their humanity.

Because of this paternalistic compromise, Genovese argues, slaveholders were locked into continuous patterns of interaction with and reaction to their slaves, which could not have left them unaware of the strength of the slaves' marital and family ties. The comments of slaveholders to the contrary, Genovese dismisses these as racist propaganda used by masters to rationalize not living up to their own paternalistic ideals.

Genovese points out that by hunting, fishing, and trapping, as well as by working the garden plots, slave husbands contributed much more to the upkeep of their families than they are usually given credit for. He argues therefore that the role of slave men in their families was not as tenuous as previously believed. In addition, he says that no matter how many slave women and children were abused by their masters, many more would have been if male slaves had not been willing to risk their lives in order to protect their women and children and if masters had not known that they would do so. Most importantly for our purposes he says: "Masters not only saw the bonds between husbands and wives, parents and children, they also saw the bond between nieces and nephews and aunts and uncles and especially between brothers and sisters" (1978:38).

Using records collected by their masters, Gutman (1976) has attempted to demonstrate that slaves living in geographically distant places, working different types of plantations, and having different daily relations with their masters all shared important beliefs indicated by similarities in their domestic arrangements, kin networks, marital rules, and naming practices. Though he somewhat casually accepts the notion of "Africanisms," (a la the compromise position), Gutman does not account for these similarities in terms of direct African survivals. Nor does he suggest that they were copied from masters. Based on the analysis of records collected by the Freedman's Bureau, Gutman's findings that many slave marriages were long and enduring are not inconsistent with those of Fogel and Engerman. Gutman suggests, however, that the durability of the conjugal ties among slaves should not be credited to the interests and efforts of their masters, but rather to internal slave beliefs. "A single South Carolina slave birth register which makes clear the extent of familial and kin networks among Afro-American slaves and shows that their development depended primarily upon the adaptive capacities of several closely related slave generations is reason enough to put aside mimetic theories of Afro-American slave culture and to describe instead how common slave sexual, marital, familial, and social choices were shaped by a neglected cumulative slave experience" (1976:45).

For Gutman, the question of survivals has clearly become not whether they exist, but what role they played in the development of Afro-American culture; how freshly enslaved Africans violently detached from their own cultures and homelands retained enough commonality to create a new culture in America. Gutman suggests that it was the enlarged slave kin network which became the basis for developing black communities.

Though placing much more emphasis on African influence, Nobles (1974) describes this adaptive process as "retribalization." According to him, the unifying commonality of West African societies was an "ethos" and its guiding principles. This ethos stressed the survival of the tribe (which was in effect synonymous with the community and the family) and that individual identity was derived from the tribe. In the face of their separation from their traditional tribes and identities, enslaved Africans created new communities and new identities guided by the same "ethosic" principles. That these principles continued to guide African behavior and beliefs in the United States is testified to by the emergence of extended kin networks and communities. Enslaved Africans had not copied the culture of their masters nor recreated any specific African culture. They had, Nobles claims, by 1860 reorganized themselves in a manner consistent with the African ethos. This ethos not only survived the Middle Passage and New World slavery, but from Nobles' point of view continues to determine the peculiar form of black families and the relational pattern they express.

Sudarkasa (1981) argues that to attempt to explain the origins of black family patterns solely in terms of African survivals or in terms of the experience of slavery is to deal with a false dichotomy. Sudarkasa also writes, "It is possible to argue that even though the constraints of slavery did prohibit the replication of African lineage ('clan') and family life in America, the principles on which these kin groups were based, and the values underlying them, led to the emergence of variants of African family life in the form of extended families which developed among the enslaved Blacks in America" (1981:39).

Frazier felt that with the advent of Emancipation the

family lives of blacks became even more disorganized than they were during the period of slavery. He felt that Emancipation, which removed prior constraints on the slaves[3] physical mobility, led many of the freedmen and women to abandon whatever families they had known and move about in search of excitement. Gutman (1976) on the other hand argues that this movement of individuals represented an attempt to reconstitute families which had been previously separated.

Frazier felt that for the majority of blacks, continued economic deprivation and social isolation would mean the continuation of family patterns based on ''folk tradition.'' He felt that the bonds between men and women remained casual and that the ''family'' often consisted of a woman, her unmarried daughter, and her daughter's children.

Even during this time period, however, Frazier felt that there was a second stream of family development among blacks. He felt that those black men who were able to rise above the impoverished condition of the masses, especially those who were able to acquire real property, were also able to establish themselves as the heads of families which were stable because they were nuclear and patriarchal.

Very little is known about how black extended families survived from the end of slavery until their modern day ''rediscovery.'' In large measure this is due to the fact that recent writers, interested in this time period, have focused on testing Frazier's earlier hypotheses using census data.[4] The problems and rewards of this methodology are clearly reflected in a study of urban black families of the nineteenth century. ''No attempt was made to establish kinship patterns since this is virtually impossible to detect from the census in a consistent way. Some cases, however, were apparent. For example, the Peterson family in Cincinnati's Ward 18 in 1880 included four separate families living in the same building, the father and his three married sons, all with their families. All four families were listed as separate households'' (Lammermeier, 1973:454).

Sudarkasa (1981) claims that after slavery some of the corporate functions of African lineages re-emerged when some black extended families became the collective owners of property.[5] In fact Barnes (1981) who interviewed middle-class black Atlanta families between September 1969 and August 1970 reported finding one family that traces the origin of its ''Cousins Club'' back to 1904. Other ongoing research which supplements census data with other types of archival data and oral histories will surely shed additional light on how the black extended family functioned during these years.

Until recently most students of the black family followed the tradition of Frazier in which concern with the effects of plantation slavery on the family lives of black people is followed by concern about the effects of urbanization and industrialization. This concern takes as its starting point the fact of rapid black urbanization. ''In 1910, 73 percent of the nation's Negro population lived in rural America, 91 percent in the South. By 1960, 73 percent lived in urban America and only 60 percent in the South. Within half a century the Negro abandoned his Southern rural past for life in a city, located more often than not in the North'' (Willhelm, 1970:15). Chicago was the final destination for many of these migrants, and several attempts have been made to delineate their impact on the development of the black community and/or family in Chicago. In the next chapter we look at some of these works in an attempt to understand why the Northern urban environment has not had a totally devastating effect on black involvement with the extended kin.

Chapter 9
In the City

IT has become *de rigueur* to point out that a black, Jean Baptiste DuSable, was "Checagou's" original settler. Prior to 1910, however, less than 2 percent of the city's population was black (Spear, 1967). Most students of the black family in Chicago ignore the increase in the black population which occurred between 1890 and 1915 (when, Spear points out, it increased from less than fifteen to more than fifty thousand) and concentrate on what has come to be called the Great Migration.

For the city of Chicago the Great Migration meant a 128 percent increase in the Negro population between 1910 and 1920. This increase was the result of both "pushes" and "pulls." During World War I manufacturing output increased, but immigration from Europe came to a standstill. In order to meet the demand for labor northern firms recruited in the South. Economic stagnation in the cotton-producing South, brought on by a series of floods and boll weevil infestations, provided the push, while job opportunities and the promise of an escape from the South's system of "Jim Crow" provided the pull. Together they promoted an out migration from the South.

E. Franklin Frazier believed that this flood of urban migrants included two very different streams of blacks. One stream carried those men and women with backgrounds embedded in the "folk tradition." Frazier felt that these people did not come from stable patriarchal homes and were not interested in creating binding marital ties.

Frazier thought that the other stream was composed of those blacks whose families had been free Negroes during slavery or who had discovered economic opportunity during and after Reconstruction. This stream, according to Frazier, included men who, because of their economic position, had established "stable families." These men either brought their families to the city with them or intended to do so.

Once in the city, however, both streams found themselves facing a similar set of problems. First, not only was the housing available to blacks located in the most dilapidated sections of town, but even in these areas it was scarce and expensive. Frazier noted that one "family" often had to take in another "family" in order to pay the rent. Second, there was the problem of income. Jobs were plentiful during World War I, but in the 1920s manufacturing output declined, and employers returned to their old hiring practices: blacks were the last hired and the first fired. Blacks were hit hard by the Depression and the shortage of jobs became even more critical. Black men found themselves out of work without marketable skills

TABLE 9.1.
Black population in Chicago, 1850–1970.

Date	Total Population	Black Population	Percent Black	Percent Increase Total Population	Percent Increase Black Population
1850	29,963	323	1.1		
1860	109,260	955	0.9	265	196
1870	298,977	3,691	1.2	174	286
1880	503,185	6,480	1.1	68	75
1890	1,099,850	14,271	1.3	119	120
1900	1,698,575	30,150	1.9	54	111
1910	2,185,283	44,103	2.0	29	46
1920	2,701,705	109,458	4.1	24	148
1930	3,376,438	233,903	6.9	25	114
1940	3,396,808	277,731	8.2	00.6	18
1950	3,620,962	492,265	13.6	06	77
1960	3,550,404	812,637	22.9	– 01.9	65
1970	3,369,359	1,102,620	32.7	– 05	35

Sources: 1850–1930: A. H. Spear, *Black Chicago*, 1967.
1940: S. C. Drake and H. Cayton, *Black Metropolis*, 1970.
1950–1960: K. E. Taeuber and A. F. Taeuber, *Negroes in Cities*, 1965.
1970: *Chicago Statistical Abstract*, Part 1, Dept. of Development and Planning, City of Chicago.

145

and unable to support their families. In Frazier's view, this set of circumstances inevitably led to high rates of illegitimacy and family dissolution among blacks.

Frazier predicted trends for the future which reflected his belief in the ultimate assimilation of blacks into the mainstream of American society and his two-stream theory. On the one hand, diminishing opportunities in southern agriculture would force more and more blacks into cities. Once there, they would find themselves impoverished, ignorant, and segregated. They would be unable to earn enough money or find sufficient housing to maintain a family. Since the majority of blacks were in this category, Frazier saw one trend which led toward increasing family instability.

On the other hand, Frazier thought that a more differentiated social structure was going to develop among blacks in cities. More Negroes would obtain an education and qualify for high-paying jobs. The expanding population of blacks would provide a market for goods and services produced and/or sold by other blacks. These expanded economic opportunities would insure the growth of a black middle class—a class which would in Frazier's view rapidly adopt the stable family norms of white society.

In his doctoral dissertation, written prior to the larger study and entitled *The Negro Family in Chicago* (1932), Frazier attempted to validate his two-stream theory. He felt that current formulations about blacks failed to realize that "the social history of the Negro reveals the fundamental distinction between the loose family organization, based on habits and affection, which was characteristic among the slaves and among the rural folk Negro and the well-organized, institutional families which developed among the Negroes who were free before the

Civil War and their descendents." Frazier pointed out that in Chicago the Negro community had expanded southward from the center of the city along State Street, cutting across several of the zones marking the expansion of Chicago. He says, "It was logical to assume that if the processes of selection and segregation operated according to Burgess' theory of urban expansion, the processes of selection and segregation should be reflected in the Negro community" (1964:205).

The black belt, which at that time extended from Twelfth Street to Sixty-third Street and was bounded on the west by Wentworth Avenue and on the east by Cottage Grove, was divided on the basis of census tracts into seven zones. Using case materials in conjunction with the ecological analysis, Frazier attempted to show how over time "the disorganization and reorganization of Negro family life are part of the processes of selection and segregation of those elements of the Negro population which have become emancipated from the masses" (1964:405).

Frazier concluded that the demographic and social differences of the populations within these zones indicated that they did provide a means for measuring the process of selection and segregation. Moving out from the center of the city there was a decline in the number of males, in the proportion of the population which was illiterate, and in the proportion of family heads which were born in the South. Conversely there was an increase in the proportion of males in high status occupations and in the number of mulattoes (except in the third zone in which the obstacle of the cabarets and black-and-tan clubs was found).

Frazier also saw, moving outward from the center of the city, a progressive stabilization of family life. This stabilization was measured in terms of the increase in the

TABLE 9.2.
*Indexes of segregation for Chicago,
1940–1970.*

Year	Segregation Index
1940	95.0
1950	92.1
1960	92.6
1970	93.0

Sources: 1940–1960: K. E. Taeuber and A. F. Taeuber, *Negroes in Cities,*
  1965.
  1970: *Where Blacks Live,* Chicago Urban League, 1978.

proportion of married men, the decrease in the proportion of female-headed ''families,'' and most importantly
an increase in the proportion of Negro families that
owned their own homes. Frazier also saw a decrease in the
degree of ''family'' disorganization. There were regular
decreases in the percent of families that came to charities
for aid and the issuance of warrants for nonsupport and
desertion. There was a decline in the rates of illegitimacy,
and in both adult and juvenile delinquency. Frazier felt
that not only had he demonstrated that Burgess' theory
worked for a segregated minority group, but also that it
was a serious mistake to treat the Negro population as a
homogeneous mass.

  By the time Drake and Cayton turned their attention to ''Black Metropolis,'' it was a city within a city, ''a
narrow strip of land, seven miles in length and one-half
mile in width, where more than 300,000 Negroes are
packed solidly'' (1970:12). Drake and Cayton never suggested that the residential encapsulation of blacks ren-

dered them a homogeneous mass. They argued rather for
a conceptualization of the distribution of socioeconomic
status within black Chicago which took the form of a
three-tiered pyramid. They argued that 65 percent of the
population could be seen as working or lower class.
Though they go on to complicate the tripartite scheme
with notions about the attitudinal and behavioral orien-
tations of families and individuals, even Drake and Cayton point out "the limited success that the people of
Bronzeville have had in sorting themselves out into broad
community areas which might be designated as 'lower
class' and 'middle class' " (1970:658).

By 1957 Frazier had reconsidered the effects of occupational differentiation on the social structure of the
black community. As he had predicted, the expanding
population of urban blacks had slowly given rise to a
black middle class. This class was comprised primarily of
wage earners and salaried professionals and contained
only a small portion of the black population. "About
one-sixth of the Negro men in the United States are employed in occupations which identify them with the *Black
Bourgeoisie*" (Frazier, 1962:27). Frazier saw the black
bourgeoisie as "lacking a cultural tradition and rejecting
identification with the Negro masses on the one hand,
and suffering from the contempt of the white world on
the other" (1962:27). And while he criticized the black
middle class for living in a world of make-believe and
engaging in conspicuous consumption, he saw the existence of these characteristics as a consequence of racial discrimination and racial segregation.

In contemporary Bronzeville the people have still
had only limited success in sorting themselves out into
broad community areas on the basis of social class. Burgess' processes of selection and segregation have certainly

TABLE 9.3.
Population by race of the community areas in which the Niles, Edmonds, Baker, and Jones family households are located, 1970–1975.

Community Area	1970 Population					1975 Population				
	Total	White No.	%	Nonwhite No.	%	Total	White No.	%	Nonwhite No.	%
25. Austin	127,981	84,917	66.4	43,064	33.6	113,587	43,049	37.9	70,538	62.1
29. North Lawndale	94,772	2,984	3.1	91,788	96.9	74,501	2,682	3.6	71,819	96.4
41. Hyde Park	33,559	21,516	64.1	12,043	35.9	29,365	15,740	53.6	13,625	46.4
42. Woodlawn	53,814	1,929	3.6	51,815	96.4	42,322	1,481	3.5	40,841	96.5
43. South Shore	80,660	24,123	29.9	56,537	70.1	71,092	7,180	10.1	63,912	89.9
54. Riverdale	15,018	757	5.0	14,261	95.0	13,041	483	3.7	12,558	96.3
56. Garfield Ridge	42,998	39,272	91.3	3,726	8.7	44,442	39,109	88.0	5,333	12.0
67. West Englewood	61,910	31,624	51.1	30,286	48.9	57,061	7,931	13.9	49,130	86.1
69. Greater Grand Crossing	54,414	814	1.5	53,600	98.5	48,984	343	0.7	48,641	99.3
71. Auburn-Gresham	68,854	21,282	30.9	47,572	69.1	62,284	2,803	4.5	59,481	95.5
75. Morgan Park	31,016	16,120	52.0	14,896	48.0	30,263	13,104	43.3	17,519	56.7

Source: "Chicago Community Areas by Race Population Estimates, 1975," United Way of Metropolitan Chicago SCAN (Aug. 1979).

not become color blind. It has been estimated that in 1940, 95 percent of all blacks in the city of Chicago would have to move in order to achieve a random distribution of households (Taeuber and Taeuber, 1965); in 1970 this percentage was estimated at 93 percent (Chicago Urban League, 1978).

Not only have the indices of segregation remained fairly stable over time but so also have the basic patterns which define where blacks may live in the city. With a 1970 population of more than 1,110,000 the black community of Chicago no longer occupies "a narrow strip of land." The continued influx of migrants from the South during the 1950s and 1960s saw the addition of the West Side and led to the popular characterization of the black community as an "L"—if one stands just north of downtown Chicago looking south, the short leg of the "L" is the West Side and the long leg the South Side. In 1970 it was no longer a neat "L." "The sections of the city to which black Chicagoans are generally confined have grown to a gigantic size during the past decades, increasing the racial isolation in which most families must live" (Chicago Urban League, 1978:1). As residents of the black community have continued to migrate toward the western and southern ends of the city they have still had only limited success in sorting themselves out by social class. Census data taken in 1970 for Chicago indicate that though more than 50 percent of the black population lived in low-income neighborhoods (contiguous census tracts in which more than 20 percent of the families had incomes less than the poverty level), only 20 percent of the black families in the city had incomes which placed them below the poverty threshhold.

In an investigation of the residential contiguity of

socioeconomic status groups in the white and black population of the entire Chicago Standard Metropolitan Statistical Area (SMSA) in 1970 Erbe found that the socioeconomic composition of neighborhoods in which white and black middle-class families live in the Chicago SMSA differs dramatically. "For the black middle-class residential segregation by socioeconomic status means living in neighborhoods with occupational, educational, and income level about that of all blacks in the Chicago Standard Metropolitan Statistical Area SMSA. It may mean the avoidance of the inner ghetto and public housing. It does not mean isolation from the Black lower class" (1975:811–12).

From the Martins' (1978) viewpoint, urban life is less conducive to the maintenance of the extended family structure than small town or rural life. They argue that because housing sufficiently large enough to contain the multigenerational family units cannot be found in urban areas, extended family members are forced to live apart, and as a result family solidarity is usually diminished. They imply that this is particularly true when differences in socioeconomic status are involved: "Though 'better off' extended family members find 'decent' places to live, the 'worse off' often settle for some of the worst housing in the city" (1978:86). They also argue that the urban environment exposes the family members to a greater risk of adopting individualistic values which are at variance with the mutual aid thrust of the extended family system.

In this work I have described some cases where blacks who differ in socioeconomic status find themselves not only encapsulated in the same "community" but also members of the same family. I do not mean to suggest that residential segregation is responsible for black involvement with the extended kin. I do mean to suggest that residential segregation by race has mediated the impact of the urban environment on involvement with the extended kin. In her study of kin relations of Londoners, for example, Elizabeth Bott (1957) found that differences in socioeconomic status did have an inhibiting effect on the frequency of interaction between kin. This relationship, however, was mediated through residential proximity. Those individuals who had been mobile had left the old neighborhood and were less accessible to their kin. The existence of residential segregation may have had an opposite effect on black involvement with the extended kin.

In the families I studied, mobiles may or may not live near the rest of their family. Unless they were doing extremely well they remained within the black community. In 1978–1979 the component households of the families described here were distributed over eleven community areas. In 1975 only two of these community areas were less than 50 percent black. The statistics at the level of the community area do not tell the entire story. Almost everyone of the households studied was located on a block which was entirely black. The only exceptions to this were the Hyde Park block where Lettie Niles lived and, interestingly enough, the block in Lawndale where the Edmonds lived. Mrs. Niles' block contained an unascertainable mixture of black, white, and other races, while one white family remained on the Edmonds' block.

Even in those cases where members of these families were relatively isolated in a geographical sense from the other members of their own family, they were not necessarily isolated from others with similar characteristics.

Ann Baker and her husband, Tom, for example, lived in a six-flat apartment building where three of the other households were welfare dependent. Sharon Baker lived in a completely black section tucked away in one corner of a largely white community area. Sharon and her husband were extremely proud of their small, four bedroom bungalow. The houses on both sides of them were not being purchased by similar conjugal pairs, but by women heading households. One of these women had seven children and a history of welfare dependence. Sharon says, "That woman always puts me in mind of Jean. How they make it with those children is beyond me."

Mobile members of contemporary urban black extended families may, as the Martins suggest, want (1) to share in the material affluence of urban society; (2) a piece of the political and economic action of urban society, and (3) to be functional in a scientifically oriented world. It does not mean as the Martins suggest that "they want to go it alone" (1978, 100).

"Alone" is not how the mobile members of the families I studied wanted to be. They certainly pictured themselves with a part of the "American Dream." In their dream, however, the nice single-family home and the two cars in the garage did not exclude sharing with mothers, fathers, brothers, sisters, nieces, nephews, or even cousins. In the city, they still believe that sharing with kin is proper.

Mobiles who continue to be involved with their extended kin certainly gain something from involvement with their less well-off kin. They clearly gain some respect for their achievements. In the eyes of the wider society the individuals described here as mobile may not have accomplished very much. The jobs they have, and of which they are very proud, are not seen as prestigious, and the wider society affords them little chance for status. The members of their families, however, understand the problems involved in obtaining and keeping any type of steady and gainful employment. The other members of these families understand the obstacles that mobiles have overcome and accord them some respect for their efforts and achievements. In the words of Ann Baker, "You cannot appreciate where I am unless you understand where I have come from."

It is through continued involvement with their kin, then, that these individuals maintain a sense of self and a sense of self-worth. Continued involvement with their kin also allows these individuals to reject some of the stereotypical images of black families. They can see, for example, that the secretary, the telephone operator, the keypunch operator, the librarian, and the police clerk were reared in the same household as two second-generation welfare recipients. They understand that this refutes the notion that poor black families are incapable of imparting the value of work to their members.

After spending a year observing these families, I came to have some understanding of how it is that black families in the urban environment transmit from generation to generation the knowledge that sharing between and among kin constitutes proper behavior. In each of these families, I often observed children attempting to replicate, point by point, the behaviors of adults toward one another as they went about the conduct of their daily affairs without consciously attempting to provide role models for children. In some instances, the adults were pleased with what they saw when children imitated them. In other instances, adults were forced to deal with imitative behavior which portrayed them violating the norms. Examples from two families can serve to illustrate this point.

The Edmonds Family: Cousins and Clothes

ONE Saturday evening I visited with Mrs. Edmonds in her apartment. Salena and her children were also present. While we talked, Karen came in. For forty-five minutes Karen continuously sighed and moved from one part of the apartment to another. Finally Mrs. Edmonds could not take it any longer and asked Karen to please tell us what her problem was. Karen explained that Ed had promised to take her to a party that night but she simply didn't have a thing to wear.

Salena stood up, collected her children and coat, and said, "Come on down to my house 'cousin,' I'll give you something to wear." What ensued was not the mere supplying of a single outfit. For more than an hour, Salena pulled clothes out of her closet and Karen tried them on. While their mothers went through this process "the girls" played and made an occasional comment on the garments being examined. When Karen and Salena had finished, they had created on Salena's bed three mounds of clothes. The first pile contained clothes that fit Salena but were too large for Karen to wear. The women hung these back in the closet and dismissed them from further consideration. The second group of clothes consisted of those that both women could wear. Salena invited Karen to wear any of these clothes but explained that they had to be returned. In the third stack were those clothes that were too small for Salena but were the right size for Karen. Salena told Karen she could both wear and keep any clothes in this last set.

About a week after the above incident, I was having coffee with Karen in her apartment when Nicole and Tasha came out of a bedroom. Karen told them to go back and get dressed. Tasha pointed out that she had only the clothes that she had worn from her house the day before, that these clothes were dirty, and that she had no intention of putting them back on. Nicole responded, ''Come on 'cousin,' I'll give you something to wear.'' Once again what followed was not a single garment operation. Nicole began taking clothes from her closet and Tasha began trying them on. When they were finished Tasha had something to put on and something to take home. Piled neatly on Nicole's bed were three groups of clothes.

The Niles Family: Whiskey in the Basket

ONE afternoon, I accompanied Louise Niles and her four-year-old daughter, Tacquita, on a visit to Louise's sister, Brenda. As Brenda opened the door for us, we all saw her five-year-old Tracey stuff a bag of potato chips under the covers of her doll cradle. There was really nothing for Brenda to do but to tell Tracey to bring the chips back out and share them with her cousin, Tacquita. Once the girls were munching placidly, however, Brenda was still not satisfied and asked Tracey why she had tried to hide the chips when she saw Tacquita at the door. ''For the same reason, Mommie,'' Tracey responded, ''that when they knocked on the door you put your whiskey in the basket." Louise then walked over to the large wicker basket that Tracey was pointing to, took off the top and pulled out an almost full quart of expensive scotch!

Children were seldom punished and often rewarded with praise for imitative behavior that was consistent with the norm. Parents or other adults often stepped in to make sure that the exchanges between children did not surpass the boundaries of "good sense." In the first example given above, the transfer of clothes from Nicole to Tasha was not complete until both mothers had gotten together and re-sorted their stacks. Both girls were then rewarded for their exemplary behavior with praise. Mrs. Edmonds was especially effusive not only in telling Nicole that she was "good girl" for passing the clothes on to Tasha before they "just got too little for anybody," but also in telling Tasha what a great person she was for so willingly accepting her cousin's hand-me-downs.

The responses of adults to imitative behavior that portrayed them violating the norms associated with kin sharing behavior were quite different. More often than not the child would be punished. This was especially true if other kin were present to witness the incident and left soon after it occurred. The punishment was often accompanied by a stern admonition to "Do as I say, not as I do." In the example given above, Brenda Niles insisted that her young daughter had misinterpreted her motivation for putting the whiskey in the basket. "I didn't know it was ya'll. I thought it was just them people from downstairs. If I don't watch them, they'll eat and drink up everything I got, and they ain't never got nothing." Once Louise and Tacquita left for home, Tracey received another lecture and a sound spanking. The punishment appeared to be as much for reporting her mother's behavior as for duplicating it.

In each of these families, correcting or contradicting one's mother in the presence of others called for an immediate response. No form of unacceptable behavior, however, always required a spanking. The adults in these families were constantly demonstrating that they could improvise on the "old fashioned whipping." When the offending behavior was explicitly kin related, the entire family could often be called upon to provide the proper response. This was demonstrated in the Baker family with "Roger and the Meat" (chapter 5).

Each of these families was constantly trying to instill in its children the notion that to share was to have. This was easily seen in those instances where the candy bar that could not be shared was taken away, where the bicycle that no other child in the family could ride was locked up, and where the television set that could not show enough channels to make everyone happy was turned off. The notion of sharing extended beyond the realm of material things and into the relationships between people. This can be seen in the instance reported in chapter 4 where Steve Edmonds demonstrates to his niece that their cousin has just as much right to his time and attention as she does.

In none of these families did the adults simply "lay back" and wait for children to need correction. In each family adults participated actively rather than simply reactively in the socialization of children. This active participation as well as the emphasis placed on the imitative process could be seen in the way family members consciously set out to provide children with adult role models. In each of these families there was some person (or persons) whose kin-related behavior made them either somebody to "be like" or somebody "not to be like."

In the Baker family, for example, Ann, Dean, and Maxie all find themselves in the position of being someone that children are told to look up to and to try to be like. Ann and Dean find themselves in this position both because they have managed to acquire some of the accoutrements of a middle-class lifestyle, including spare cash, and because they continue to share both their time and their resources with their kin. These two sisters, like Steve Edmonds, certainly serve to introduce younger members of their family to the world of work. Maxie occupies this position because even though she has very little, she would "give you the shirt off her back." WeeWee Baker will be hearing the story of how Ann and Maxie assisted in her birth for the rest of her life. She will constantly be reminded that their behavior toward her was proper and will be encouraged to be as considerate of future kin as they were of her.

Christine Baker, on the other hand, is presented to the children as antisocial and selfish and under no circumstances to be emulated. According to her sisters, Christine's "antisocial nature" is illustrated by the fact that she visits no one regularly except her mother and by the fact that she has even moved without informing them of her new address. Christine's selfishness, her sisters claim, is indicated by the fact that though she always "wants" and often "needs" something she is generally reluctant to give anything up and seldom does so graciously. According to her family, then, Christine provides the best example of how little one can share and still be a member of the family.

Notes

Chapter 1.   Introduction

1. Unfortunately, the nature of my observations does not allow me to make this additional step. Perhaps the best I can hope to do is allow those who suggest a return to the extended family to see that they run the risk of blaming black families for their members' failure to achieve the American Dream. Perhaps the ideological process described by Ryan as "Blaming the Victim" is so deeply entrenched in the American psyche that no matter what external structures or internal processes are described as being characteristic of black families, the conclusions drawn will always include "Is it any wonder the Negroes cannot achieve equality? From such families!" (Ryan, 1971:5). What I can be sure of is that blaming the victim always simplifies policy decisions: if we are speaking in the terminology of the 1960s, then a "deteriorating" Negro family must be "strengthened"; if blacks must isolate themselves from their kin in order to be mobile, then some way must be found to encourage them to disengage from kin; if adverse political and economic conditions threaten, then blacks must return to the family patterns of the past. Either way, it is suggested, what must be changed in order to promote the welfare of blacks is the black family itself. If, on the other hand, we recognize that the black underclass did not create itself and does not perpetuate itself through its family organization, we can also realize that what must be changed are factors external to the family. The black underclass was created through the systematic efforts of whites to suppress blacks; denying

them "access to valued and scarce resources through various ingenious schemes of racial exploitation, discrimination, and segregation, schemes that were reinforced by elaborate ideologies of racism" (Wilson, 1978:1). The existence of the black underclass is perpetuated by the vestiges of traditional segregation and discrimination coupled with a politically motivated neglect of the problems faced by blacks in dealing with basic structural shifts in the economy.

2. I refer, for example, to the April 5, 1982, *Newsweek* that bears on its cover the title "Reagan's America . . . And the Poor Get Poorer," and to the CBS Report entitled "People Like Us."

3. The recognition that ideology and theory are not isolated from each other is certainly not limited to the study of black families. "Historically, American sociologists have employed three distinct theoretical interpretations of pluralism. The theories of assimilation, amalgamation, and cultural pluralism have each, in turn, provided answers to the question: What kind of long term social process emerges in a pluralistic society? Yet the intriguing thing about these three theories is that they did not originate in the halls of science. . . . Assimilation, amalgamation, and cultural pluralism have appeared as successive ideological interpretations of the meaning of American history." [Newman, 1973:51]

4. Even students of blacks in the Caribbean have not studied the relations between kin who differ in socioeconomic status. Either blacks as a group are seen as being relegated to the lowest rung of the status hierarchy, so that their family life can be studied with socioeconomic status as a constant, or differences in family patterns are seen as changing with social class.

Chapter 2.   Identifying the Families

1. In this sense they were much more perceptive than one of my faculty advisors, who kept insisting that if I didn't like the ghetto, I should just move out.

2. Valentine (1978) recounts having her stereo system stolen while living in Blackston. My apartment was broken into so many times that I began to leave a note for the burglars asking them, by name, for their share of the rent. When they decided to break into the apartment when they knew that I was at home, I knew that it was time to leave Austin.

3. The University of Illinois at Chicago Circle.

4. Wilson, on the other hand, says that "within the lower class is a heterogeneous grouping—an underclass population which represents the very bottom of the economic hierarchy and not only includes those lower class workers whose income falls below the poverty level but also the more or less permanent welfare recipients, the long term unemployed, and those who have dropped out of the labor market" (1978:156).

5. These family names, as well as those of individual members, are pseudonyms, designed to protect the anonymity of informants and their families.

Chapter 7.   Commonalities and Differences

1. I did learn, however, that concentrating on the present was not the key to understanding the relationships between members of these families. The patterns of reciprocity were often explained by them as reaching far back in time.

2. I will certainly not attempt to review the entire literature on reciprocity. Sahlins' scheme is used here because whatever its problems, it provided the clearest way of describing the behavior that I was observing. According to Sahlins, "gift exchange" is a classic example of balanced reciprocity.

3. The Jones family did appear to engage in illegal activities to a greater extent than the other families.

Chapter 8.   Origins and Consequences

1. It must also be remembered that Frazier was attempting to refute arguments that claimed that because blacks were biologically and/or culturally inferior to whites, they could never be meaningfully integrated into the mainstream of American society (Frazier, 1947).

2. Concern with extended kinship among whites, on the other hand, had its origins in the abstract intellectual and often semantic debates about the nature of the relationship between the familial and economic systems of a society. The participants in these debates tend to give the economic system priority as the independent or causal variable and focus their attention on exactly how the resulting kinship system should be described and its family forms classified.

3. The literature that argues this position for white families is quite large and will not be reviewed here. The interested reader is referred to Adams, 1970.

4. Studies that have focused on household composition during the antebellum and early postbellum periods have found a rather high degree of marital stability (Pleck, 1972; Hershberg, 1971–1972; Lammermeier, 1973; Furstenberg, et al., 1975; Shifflet, 1975). The work of Furstenberg, Hershberg, and Model (1975) suggests, however that racial differences in the number of female-headed households had already appeared by 1880.

5. I am currently engaged in research designed to explore the development of Afro-American family patterns in an all-black community between Emancipation and the Great Depression.

References

Adams, Bert. "Isolation, Function and Beyond: American Kinship in the 1960s." *Journal of Marriage and the Family* (1970) 32:575–97.

Allen, Walter R. "The Search for Applicable Theories of Black Family Life," *Journal of Marriage and the Family* (1978) 40:117–30.

Aschenbrenner, Joyce. "Extended Families Among Black Americans." *Journal of Comparative Family Studies* (1973) 4:257–68.

Aschenbrenner, Joyce. *Lifelines: Black Families in Chicago.* New York: Holt, Rinehart and Winston, 1975.

Askin, Steve. "New Poverty Traps 600,000 Chicagoans—Permanently." *Chicago Reporter,* Feb. 1980, 9(2).

Ball, Donald. "The 'Family' as a Sociological Problem: Conceptualization of the Taken for Granted as Prologue to Social Problems Analysis." *Social Problems* (1972) 19:295–307.

Barnes, Annie S. "The Black Kinship System." *Phylon* (Dec. 1981) 42(4):369–80.

Bernard, Jesse. *Marriage and the Family Among Negroes.* Englewood Cliffs, N.J.: Prentice-Hall, 1966.

Billingsley, Andrew. *Black Families in White America.* Englewood Cliffs, N.J.: Prentice-Hall, 1968.

Blassingame, John W. *The Slave Community.* New York: Oxford University Press, 1972.

Blumberg, Rae L., and Maria P. Garcia. "The Political Economy of the Mother-Child Household." In R. Winch, ed., *Familial Organization:*

The Quest for Determinants. New York: Free Press, 1977. Pp. 144–75.

Bogue, Donald J. *Principles of Demography.* New York: Wiley, 1969.

Bott, Elizabeth. *Family and Social Network.* London: Tavistock Pubns., 1957.

Bryce-LaPorte, Roy S. "The American Slave Plantation and Our Heritage of Communal Deprivation." *American Scientist* (1969) 12:2–8.

Clarke, John H. "The Black Family in Historical Perspective." *Journal of Afro-American Issues* (1975) 3:336–42.

Davidson, Basil. *The African Slave Trade.* Boston: Little Brown, 1961.

Dodson, Jualynne. Beverly Hills, Calif.: Sage Pubns., 1981.

Drake, St. Clair, and Horace Cayton. *Black Metropolis.* New York: Harcourt, Brace and World, 1970. Originally published in 1945.

DuBois, W. E. B. *The Negro American Family.* Atlanta, Ga.: Atlanta University Press, 1908.

Elkins, Stanley M. *Slavery.* Chicago: University of Chicago Press, 1959.

Erbe, Brigette M. "Race and Socioeconomic Segregation." *American Sociological Review* (1975) 40:801–12.

Farley, Reynolds. *Growth of the Black Population.* Chicago: Markham, 1970.

Feagin, Joe R. "The Kinship Ties of Negro Urbanites." *Social Science Quarterly* (1968) 49:660–65.

Fogel, Robert W., and Stanley L. Engerman. *Time on the Cross.* Boston: Little Brown, 1974.

Frazier, E. Franklin. *The Negro Family in Chicago.* Chicago: University of Chicago Press, 1932.

Frazier, E. Franklin. *The Negro Family in the United States.* Chicago: University of Chicago Press, 1966. Originally published in 1939.

Frazier, E. Franklin. "Ethnic Family Patterns: The Negro Family in the United States." *American Journal of Sociology* (May 1948) 54:433–38.

Frazier, E. Franklin. *Black Bourgeoisie.* New York: Collier, 1962. Originally published in 1957.

Frazier, E. Franklin. "The Negro Family in Chicago." In Burgess and Bogue, eds., *Contributions to Urban Sociology.* Chicago: University of Chicago Press, 1964. Pp. 404–18.

Furstenberg, Frank F., Jr., Theodor Hershberg, and John Modell. "The Origins of the Female Headed Black Family: The Impact of the Urgan Experience." *Journal of Interdisciplinary History* (1975) 6: 211–33.

Genovese, Eugene. *The Political Economy of Slavery: Studies in the Economy and Society of the Slave South.* New York: Pantheon, 1966.

Genovese, Eugene. *Roll Jordan Roll: The World the Slaves Made.* New York: Pantheon Books, 1974.

Genovese, Eugene. "The Myth of the Absent Family." In Robert Staples, ed., *The Black Family: Essays and Studies.* Belmont, Calif.: Wadsworth, 1978. Pp. 35–43.

Gonzalez, Nancy L. *Black Carib Household Structure.* Seattle: University of Washington Press, 1969.

Gonzalez, Nancy L. "Toward a Definition of Matrifocality." In Whitten and Szwed, eds., *Afro-American Anthropology: Contemporary Perspectives.* New York: Free Press, 1970. Pp. 231–43.

Green, Mitchell A. "Impact of Slavery on the Black Family: Social, Political and Economic." *Journal of Afro-American Issues* (1975) 3:343–54.

Greenfield, Sidney M. *English Rustics in Black Skin: A Study of Modern Family Forms in a Pre-Industrialized Society.* New Haven, Conn.: College and University Press, 1966.

Gutman, Herbert G. "Persistent Myths about the Afro-American Family." *Journal of Interdisciplinary History* (1975) 6:181–210.

Gutman, Herbert G. *The Black Family in Slavery and Freedom, 1750–1925.* New York: Pantheon Books, 1976.

Hersberg, Theodore. "Free Blacks in Ante-Bellum Philadelphia." *Journal of Social History* (1971–72) 5:183–290.

Herskovits, Melville J. *The Myth of the Negro Past.* Boston, Mass.: Beacon Press, 1958. Originally published in 1941.

Hill, Robert. *The Strengths of Black Families.* New York: Emerson Hall, 1971.

Hyman, Herbert H., and John S. Reed. "Black Matriarchy Reconsidered: Evidence from Secondary Analysis of Sample Surveys." *Public Opinion Quarterly* (1969) 33:345–54.

Keil, Charles. *Urban Blues.* Chicago: University of Chicago Press, 1966.

Johnson, Lenore. "The Search for Values in Black Family Research." In R. Staples, ed., *The Black Family: Essays and Studies.* Belmont, Calif.: Wadsworth, 1978.

Johnson, Lenore. "Perspectives on Black Family Empirical Research: 1965–1978." In McAdoo, ed., *Black Families.* Beverly Hills, Calif.: Sage Pubns., 1981.

Ladner, Joyce. *Tomorrow's Tomorrow: The Black Woman.* Garden City, N.J.: Doubleday, 1971.

Lammermeier, Paul J. "The Urban Black Family of the Nineteenth Century: A Study of Black Family Structure in the Ohio Valley, 1850–1880." *Journal of Marriage and the Family* (1973) 35:440–56.

Lieberman, Leonard. "The Emerging Model of the Black Family." *International Journal of Sociology of the Family* (1973) 3:10–22.

Mack, Delores E. "The Power Relationship in Black Families." *Journal of Personality and Social Psychology* Sept. 1974) 30:409–13.

Mathis, Arthur. "Contrasting Approaches to the Study of Black Families." *Journal of Marriage and the Family* (Nov. 1978) 14 (40):667–76.

Martin, Elmer P., and Joanne M. Martin. *The Black Extended Family.* Chicago: University of Chicago Press, 1978.

McAdoo, Harriette P. "Impact of the Extended Family Structure on Upward Mobility of Blacks." *Journal of Afro-American Issues* 3:291–96.

McAdoo, Harriette P. "The Ecology of Internal and External Support Systems of Black Families." Paper presented at the National Urban League Conference on Black Families, Chicago, 1977.

McAdoo, Harriette P. "Factors Related to Stability in Upwardly Mobile Black Families." *Journal of Marriage and the Family* (1978) 4(40):761–66.

McAdoo, Harriette P. "Black Kinship." *Psychology Today*. May 1979, pp. 67, 69, 70, 79, 110.

McAdoo, Harriette P. "Black Mothers and the Extended Family Support Network." In Rodgers-Rose, ed., *The Black Woman*. Beverly Hills, Calif.: Sage Pubns., 1980.

McAdoo, Harriette P. "Patterns of Upward Mobility in Black Families." In H. McAdoo, ed., *Black Families*. Beverly Hills, Calif.: Sage Pubns., 1981.

Moynihan, Daniel P. *The Negro Family: The Case for National Action*. Office of Policy Planning and Research, U.S. Dept. of Labor, 1965.

Murdock, George P. *Social Structure*. New York: Macmillan, 1949.

Newman, William M. *American Pluralism: A Study of Minority Groups and Social Theory*. New York: Harper and Row, 1973.

Nobles, Wade. "Africanity: Its Role in Black Families." *The Black Scholar*. (1974) 5:10–17.

Nobles, Wade. "Toward an Empirical and Theoretical Framework for Defining Black Families." *Journal of Marriage and the Family* (1978)40 (4):679–88.

Nobles, Wade. "African American Family Life: An Instrument of Culture." In H. McAdoo, ed., *Black Families*. Beverly Hills, Calif.: Sage Pubns., 1982.

Parsons, Talcott. "The Kinship System of the Contemporary United States." *American Anthropologist* (1943) 45:22–28.

Pleck, Elizabeth. "The Two-Parent Household: Black Family Structure in Late Nineteenth Century Boston." *Journal of Social History* (1972) 6:3–31.

Rawick, George P. *From Sundown to Sunup*. Westport, Conn.: Greenwood Press, 1972.

Sagan, Carl. *The Dragons of Eden: Speculations on the Origins of Human Intelligence*. New York: Ballantine, 1977.

Schneider, David M., and Raymond T. Smith. *Class Difference and Sex Roles in American Kinship and Family Structure*. Englewood Cliffs, N.J.: Prentice-Hall, 1973.

Sennett, Richard. *Families Against the City*. New York: Vintage Books, 1974.

Shifflett, Carndall A. "The Household Composition of Rural Black Families: Louis County, Virginia, 1880." *Journal of Interdisciplinary History* (1975) 3:234–60.

Smith, Raymond T. *The Negro Family in British Guiana: Family Structure and Social Status in the Village*. London: Routledge and Kegan Paul, 1956.

Spear, Allen H. *Black Chicago*. Chicago: University of Chicago Press, 1967.

Stack, Carol B. *All Our Kin*. New York: Harper and Row, 1974.

Stampp, Kenneth M. *The Peculiar Institution.* New York: Knopf, 1956.
Staples, Robert. "The Black Family Revisited." *Journal of Social and Behavioral Sciences* (Spring 1974) 20:65–78.
Sudarkasa, Niara. "Interpreting the African Heritage in Afro-American Family Organization." In H. McAdoo, ed., *Black Families.* Beverly Hills, Calif.: Sage Pubns., 1981.
Taeuber, Karl E., and Alma F. Taeuber. *Negroes in Cities.* Chicago: Aldine, 1965.
Tannenbaum, Frank. *Slave and Citizen.* New York: Knopf, 1946.
TenHouten, Warren D. "The Black Family: Myth and Reality." *Psychiatry* (1970) 33:145–73.
Thomas, William I., and Florian Znaniecki. *The Polish Peasant in Europe and America.* New York: Dover, 1958.
Valentine, Bettylou. *Hustling and Other Hard Work: Life Styles in the Ghetto.* New York: Free Press, 1978.
Wade, R. *Slavery in the Cities: The South 1820–1860.* London: Oxford University Press, 1964.
Watts, Lewis G. "The Middle Income Negro Family Faces Urban Renewal." In J. Feagin, ed., *The Urban Scene: Myths and Realities.* New York: Random House, 1964.
Whitten, Norman E., Jr., and John F. Szwed, eds. *Afro-American Anthropology.* New York: Free Press, 1970.
Willie, Charles V. *A New Look at Black Families.* Englewood Cliffs, N.J.: Prentice-Hall, 1974.
Willhelm, Sidney. *Who Needs the Negro?* Garden City, N.Y.: Doubleday, 1971.
Wilson, William J. *The Declining Significance of Race: Blacks and Changing American Institutions.* Chicago: University of Chicago Press, 1978.
Winch, Robert F. *Familial Organization: The Quest for Determinants.* New York: Free Press, 1977.
Wirth, Louis. "Urbanism as a Way of Life." *American Journal of Sociology* (1938) 44:1–24.
Woodson, Carter G. *The Miseducation of the Negro.* New York: AMS Press, 1977. Originally published in 1933.

Index